TABLE OF C~~ONTENTS~~

D1516383

Unless otherwise indicated, all Scripture quotations are taken from the King James Version of the Bible.
31 Greatest Chapters In The Bible
ISBN 1-56394-170-8
Copyright © 2002 by *MIKE MURDOCK*
All publishing rights belong exclusively to Wisdom International
Published by The Wisdom Center
P. O. Box 99 · Denton, Texas 76202 · 1-888-WISDOM-1 (1-888-947-3661)
Website: www.thewisdomcenter.cc

1

CREATION

GENESIS 1

1) In the beginning God created the heaven and the earth.

2) And the earth was without form, and void; and darkness was upon the face of the deep. And the Spirit of God moved upon the face of the waters.

3) And God said, Let there be light: and there was light.

4) And God saw the light, that it was good: and God divided the light from the darkness.

5) And God called the light Day, and the darkness He called Night. And the evening and the morning were the first day.

6) And God said, Let there be a firmament in the midst of the waters, and let it divide the waters from the waters.

7) And God made the firmament, and divided the waters which were under the firmament from the waters which were above the firmament: and it was so.

8) And God called the firmament Heaven. And the evening and the morning were the second

day.

9) And God said, Let the waters under the heaven be gathered together unto one place, and let the dry land appear: and it was so.

10) And God called the dry land Earth; and the gathering together of the waters called He Seas: and God saw that it was good.

11) And God said, Let the earth bring forth grass, the herb yielding seed, and the fruit tree yielding fruit after his kind, whose seed is in itself, upon the earth: and it was so.

12) And the earth brought forth grass, and herb yielding seed after his kind, and the tree yielding fruit, whose seed was in itself, after his kind: and God saw that it was good.

13) And the evening and the morning were the third day.

14) And God said, Let there be lights in the firmament of the heaven to divide the day from the night; and let them be for signs, and for seasons, and for days, and years:

15) And let them be for lights in the firmament of the heaven to give light upon the earth: and it was so.

16) And God made two great lights; the greater light to rule the day, and the lesser light to rule the night: He made the stars also.

17) And God set them in the firmament of the heaven to give light upon the earth,

18) And to rule over the day and over the night, and to divide the light from the darkness: and God saw that it was good.

19) And the evening and the morning were

the fourth day.

20) And God said, Let the waters bring forth abundantly the moving creature that hath life, and fowl that may fly above the earth in the open firmament of heaven.

21) And God created great whales, and every living creature that moveth, which the waters brought forth abundantly, after their kind, and every winged fowl after his kind: and God saw that it was good.

22) And God blessed them, saying, Be fruitful, and multiply, and fill the waters in the seas, and let fowl multiply in the earth.

23) And the evening and the morning were the fifth day.

24) And God said, Let the earth bring forth the living creature after his kind, cattle, and creeping thing, and beast of the earth after his kind: and it was so.

25) And God made the beast of the earth after his kind, and cattle after their kind, and every thing that creepeth upon the earth after his kind: and God saw that it was good.

26) And God said, Let us make man in Our image, after Our likeness: and let them have dominion over the fish of the sea, and over the fowl of the air, and over the cattle, and over all the earth, and over every creeping thing that creepeth upon the earth.

27) So God created man in His own image, in the image of God created He him; male and female created He them.

28) And God blessed them, and God said

unto them, Be fruitful, and multiply, and replenish the earth, and subdue it: and have dominion over the fish of the sea, and over the fowl of the air, and over every living thing that moveth upon the earth.

29) And God said, Behold, I have given you every herb bearing seed, which is upon the face of all the earth, and every tree, in the which is the fruit of a tree yielding seed; to you it shall be for meat.

30) And to every beast of the earth, and to every fowl of the air, and to every thing that creepeth upon the earth, wherein there is life, I have given every green herb for meat: and it was so.

31) And God saw every thing that He had made, and, behold, it was very good. And the evening and the morning were the sixth day.

Genesis 1:1-31

2

CREATION OF MAN

GENESIS 2

1) Thus the heavens and the earth were finished, and all the host of them.

2) And on the seventh day God ended His work which He had made; and He rested on the seventh day from all His work which He had made.

3) And God blessed the seventh day, and sanctified it: because that in it He had rested from all His work which God created and made.

4) These are the generations of the heavens and of the earth when they were created, in the day that the Lord God made the earth and the heavens,

5) And every plant of the field before it was in the earth, and every herb of the field before it grew: for the Lord God had not caused it to rain upon the earth, and there was not a man to till the ground.

6) But there went up a mist from the earth, and watered the whole face of the ground.

7) And the Lord God formed man of the dust of the ground, and breathed into his nostrils the breath of life; and man became a living soul.

8) And the Lord God planted a garden

eastward in Eden; and there He put the man whom He had formed.

9) And out of the ground made the Lord God to grow every tree that is pleasant to the sight, and good for food; the tree of life also in the midst of the garden, and the tree of knowledge of good and evil.

10) And a river went out of Eden to water the garden; and from thence it was parted, and became into four heads.

11) The name of the first is Pison: that is it which compasseth the whole land of Havilah, where there is gold;

12) And the gold of that land is good: there is bdellium and the onyx stone.

13) And the name of the second river is Gihon: the same is it that compasseth the whole land of Ethiopia.

14) And the name of the third river is Hiddekel: that is it which goeth toward the east of Assyria. And the fourth river is Euphrates.

15) And the Lord God took the man, and put him into the garden of Eden to dress it and to keep it.

16) And the Lord God commanded the man, saying, Of every tree of the garden thou mayest freely eat:

17) But of the tree of the knowledge of good and evil, thou shalt not eat of it: for in the day that thou eatest thereof thou shalt surely die.

18) And the Lord God said, It is not good that the man should be alone; I will make him an help meet for him.

19) And out of the ground the Lord God

formed every beast of the field, and every fowl of the air; and brought them unto Adam to see what he would call them: and whatsoever Adam called every living creature, that was the name thereof.

20) And Adam gave names to all cattle, and to the fowl of the air, and to every beast of the field; but for Adam there was not found an help meet for him.

21) And the Lord God caused a deep sleep to fall upon Adam, and he slept: and He took one of his ribs, and closed up the flesh instead thereof;

22) And the rib, which the Lord God had taken from man, made He a woman, and brought her unto the man.

23) And Adam said, This is now bone of my bones, and flesh of my flesh: she shall be called Woman, because she was taken out of Man.

24) Therefore shall a man leave his father and his mother, and shall cleave unto his wife: and they shall be one flesh.

25) And they were both naked, the man and his wife, and were not ashamed. *Genesis 2:1-25*

God's Only Pain
Is To Be Doubted-
God's Only Pleasure
Is To Be Believed.

-MIKE MURDOCK

❦ 3 ❦

10 COMMANDMENTS

EXODUS 20

1)　And God spake all these words, saying,

2)　I am the Lord thy God, which have brought thee out of the land of Egypt, out of the house of bondage.

3)　Thou shalt have no other gods before me.

4)　Thou shalt not make unto thee any graven image, or any likeness of any thing that is in heaven above, or that is in the earth beneath, or that is in the water under the earth:

5)　Thou shalt not bow down thyself to them, nor serve them:　for I the Lord thy God am a jealous God, visiting the iniquity of the fathers upon the children unto the third and fourth generation of them that hate Me;

6)　And shewing mercy unto thousands of them that love Me, and keep My commandments.

7)　Thou shalt not take the name of the Lord thy God in vain; for the Lord will not hold him guiltless that taketh His name in vain.

8)　Remember the sabbath day, to keep it holy.

9)　Six days shalt thou labour, and do all thy work:

work:

10) But the seventh day is the sabbath of the Lord thy God: in it thou shalt not do any work, thou, nor thy son, nor thy daughter, thy manservant, nor thy maidservant, nor thy cattle, nor thy stranger that is within thy gates:

11) For in six days the Lord made heaven and earth, the sea, and all that in them is, and rested the seventh day: wherefore the Lord blessed the sabbath day, and hallowed it.

12) Honour thy father and thy mother: that thy days may be long upon the land which the Lord thy God giveth thee.

13) Thou shalt not kill.

14) Thou shalt not commit adultery.

15) Thou shalt not steal.

16) Thou shalt not bear false witness against thy neighbour.

17) Thou shalt not covet thy neighbour's house, thou shalt not covet thy neighbour's wife, nor his manservant, nor his maidservant, nor his ox, nor his ass, nor any thing that is thy neighbour's.

18) And all the people saw the thunderings, and the lightnings, and the noise of the trumpet, and the mountain smoking: and when the people saw it, they removed, and stood afar off.

19) And they said unto Moses, Speak thou with us, and we will hear: but let not God speak with us, lest we die.

20) And Moses said unto the people, Fear not: for God is come to prove you, and that His fear may be before your faces, that ye sin not.

21) And the people stood afar off, and Moses drew near unto the thick darkness where God was.

22) And the Lord said unto Moses, Thus thou shalt say unto the children of Israel, Ye have seen that I have talked with you from heaven.

23) Ye shall not make with Me gods of silver, neither shall ye make unto you gods of gold.

24) An altar of earth thou shalt make unto Me, and shalt sacrifice thereon thy burnt offerings, and thy peace offerings, thy sheep, and thine oxen: in all places where I record My name I will come unto thee, and I will bless thee.

25) And if thou wilt make Me an altar of stone, thou shalt not build it of hewn stone: for if thou lift up thy tool upon it, thou hast polluted it.

26) Neither shalt thou go up by steps unto Mine altar, that thy nakedness be not discovered thereon.   *Exodus 20:1-26*

The Anointing You Respect...
Is The Anointing
That Increases In Your Life.

-MIKE MURDOCK

❧ 4 ❧

BLESSINGS AND CURSES

DEUTERONOMY 28

1) And it shall come to pass, if thou shalt hearken diligently unto the voice of the Lord thy God, to observe and to do all His commandments which I command thee this day, that the Lord thy God will set thee on high above all nations of the earth:

2) And all these blessings shall come on thee, and overtake thee, if thou shalt hearken unto the voice of the Lord thy God.

3) Blessed shalt thou be in the city, and blessed shalt thou be in the field.

4) Blessed shall be the fruit of thy body, and the fruit of thy ground, and the fruit of thy cattle, the increase of thy kine, and the flocks of thy sheep.

5) Blessed shall be thy basket and thy store.

6) Blessed shalt thou be when thou comest in, and blessed shalt thou be when thou goest out.

7) The Lord shall cause thine enemies that rise up against thee to be smitten before thy face: they shall come out against thee one way, and flee before thee seven ways.

8) The Lord shall command the blessing upon thee in thy storehouses, and in all that thou

settest thine hand unto; and He shall bless thee in the land which the Lord thy God giveth thee.

9) The Lord shall establish thee an holy people unto Himself, as He hath sworn unto thee, if thou shalt keep the commandments of the Lord thy God, and walk in His ways.

10) And all people of the earth shall see that thou art called by the name of Lord; and they shall be afraid of thee.

11) And the Lord shall make thee plenteous in goods, in the fruit of thy body, and in the fruit of thy cattle, and in the fruit of thy ground, in the land which the Lord sware unto thy fathers to give thee.

12) The Lord shall open unto thee His good treasure, the heaven to give the rain unto thy land in His season, and to bless all the work of thine hand: and thou shalt lend unto many nations, and thou shalt not borrow.

13) And the Lord shall make thee the head, and not the tail; and thou shalt be above only, and thou shalt not be beneath; if that thou hearken unto the commandments of the Lord thy God, which I command thee this day, to observe and to do them:

14) And thou shalt not go aside from any of the words which I command thee this day, to the right hand, or to the left, to go after other gods to serve them.

15) But it shall come to pass, if thou wilt not hearken unto the voice of the Lord thy God, to observe to do all His commandments and His statutes which I command thee this day; that all these curses shall come upon thee, and overtake

thee:

16) Cursed shalt thou be in the city, and cursed shalt thou be in the field.

17) Cursed shall be thy basket and thy store.

18) Cursed shall be the fruit of thy body, and the fruit of thy land, the increase of thy kine, and the flocks of thy sheep.

19) Cursed shalt thou be when thou comest in, and cursed shalt thou be when thou goest out.

20) The Lord shall send upon thee cursing, vexation, and rebuke, in all that thou settest thine hand unto for to do, until thou be destroyed, and until thou perish quickly; because of the wickedness of thy doings, whereby thou hast forsaken Me.

21) The Lord shall make the pestilence cleave unto thee, until He have consumed thee from off the land, whither thou goest to possess it.

22) The Lord shall smite thee with a consumption, and with a fever, and with an inflammation, and with an extreme burning, and with the sword, and with blasting, and with mildew; and they shall pursue thee until thou perish.

23) And thy heaven that is over thy head shall be brass, and the earth that is under thee shall be iron.

24) The Lord shall make the rain of thy land powder and dust: from heaven shall it come down upon thee, until thou be destroyed.

25) The Lord shall cause thee to be smitten before thine enemies: thou shalt go out one way against them, and flee seven ways before them: and shalt be removed into all the kingdoms of the

earth.

26) And thy carcase shall be meat unto all fowls of the air, and unto the beasts of the earth, and no man shall fray them away.

27) The Lord will smite thee with the botch of Egypt, and with the emerods, and with the scab, and with the itch, whereof thou canst not be healed.

28) The Lord shall smite thee with madness, and blindness, and astonishment of heart:

29) And thou shalt grope at noonday, as the blind gropeth in darkness, and thou shalt not prosper in thy ways: and thou shalt be only oppressed and spoiled evermore, and no man shall save thee.

30) Thou shalt betroth a wife, and another man shall lie with her: thou shalt build an house, and thou shalt not dwell therein: thou shalt plant a vineyard, and shalt not gather the grapes thereof.

31) Thine ox shall be slain before thine eyes, and thou shalt not eat thereof: thine ass shall be violently taken away from before thy face, and shall not be restored to thee: thy sheep shall be given unto thine enemies, and thou shalt have none to rescue them.

32) Thy sons and thy daughters shall be given unto another people, and thine eyes shall look, and fail with longing for them all the day long: and there shall be no might in thine hand.

33) The fruit of thy land, and all thy labours, shall a nation which thou knowest not eat up; and thou shalt be only oppressed and crushed alway:

34) So that thou shalt be mad for the sight of thine eyes which thou shalt see.

35) The Lord shall smite thee in the knees, and in the legs, with a sore botch that cannot be healed, from the sole of thy foot unto the top of thy head.

36) The Lord shall bring thee, and thy king which thou shalt set over thee, unto a nation which neither thou nor thy fathers have known; and there shalt thou serve other gods, wood and stone.

37) And thou shalt become an astonishment, a proverb, and a byword, among all nations whither the Lord shall lead thee.

38) Thou shalt carry much seed out into the field, and shalt gather but little in; for the locust shall consume it.

39) Thou shalt plant vineyards, and dress them, but shalt neither drink of the wine, nor gather the grapes; for the worms shall eat them.

40) Thou shalt have olive trees throughout all thy coasts, but thou shalt not anoint thyself with the oil; for thine olive shall cast his fruit.

41) Thou shalt beget sons and daughters, but thou shalt not enjoy them; for they shall go into captivity.

42) All thy trees and fruit of thy land shall the locust consume.

43) The stranger that is within thee shall get up above thee very high; and thou shalt come down very low.

44) He shall lend to thee, and thou shalt not lend to him: he shall be the head, and thou shalt be the tail.

45) Moreover all these curses shall come upon thee, and shall pursue thee, and overtake thee, till thou be destroyed; because thou hearkenedst not unto the voice of the Lord thy God, to keep His

commandments and His statutes which He commanded thee:

46) And they shall be upon thee for a sign and for a wonder, and upon thy seed for ever.

47) Because thou servedst not the Lord thy God with joyfulness, and with gladness of heart, for the abundance of all things;

48) Therefore shalt thou serve thine enemies which the Lord shall send against thee, in hunger, and in thirst, and in nakedness, and in want of all things: and He shall put a yoke of iron upon thy neck, until He have destroyed thee.

49) The Lord shall bring a nation against thee from far, from the end of the earth, as swift as the eagle flieth; a nation whose tongue thou shalt not understand;

50) A nation of fierce countenance, which shall not regard the person of the old, nor shew favour to the young:

51) And he shall eat the fruit of thy cattle, and the fruit of thy land, until thou be destroyed: which also shall not leave thee either corn, wine, or oil, or the increase of thy kine, or flocks of thy sheep, until he have destroyed thee.

52) And he shall besiege thee in all thy gates, until thy high and fenced walls come down, wherein thou trustedst, throughout all thy land: and he shall besiege thee in all thy gates throughout all thy land, which the Lord thy God hath given thee.

53) And thou shalt eat the fruit of thine own body, the flesh of thy sons and of thy daughters, which the Lord thy God hath given thee, in the siege, and in the straitness, wherewith thine enemies shall distress thee:

54) So that the man that is tender among you, and very delicate, his eye shall be evil toward his brother, and toward the wife of his bosom, and toward the remnant of his children which he shall leave:

55) So that he will not give to any of them of the flesh of his children whom he shall eat: because he hath nothing left him in the siege, and in the straitness, wherewith thine enemies shall distress thee in all thy gates.

56) The tender and delicate woman among you, which would not adventure to set the sole of her foot upon the ground for delicateness and tenderness, her eye shall be evil toward the husband of her bosom, and toward her son, and toward her daughter,

57) And toward her young one that cometh out from between her feet, and toward her children which she shall bear: for she shall eat them for want of all things secretly in the siege and straitness, wherewith thine enemy shall distress thee in thy gates.

58) If thou wilt not observe to do all the words of this law that are written in this book, that thou mayest fear this glorious and fearful name, The Lord Thy God;

59) Then the Lord will make thy plagues wonderful, and the plagues of thy seed, even great plagues, and of long continuance, and sore sicknesses, and of long continuance.

60) Moreover He will bring upon thee all the diseases of Egypt, which thou wast afraid of; and they shall cleave unto thee.

61) Also every sickness, and every plague, which is not written in the book of this law, them

will the Lord bring upon thee, until thou be destroyed.

62) And ye shall be left few in number, whereas ye were as the stars of heaven for multitude; because thou wouldest not obey the voice of the Lord thy God.

63) And it shall come to pass, that as the Lord rejoiced over you to do you good, and to multiply you; so the Lord will rejoice over you to destroy you, and to bring you to nought; and ye shall be plucked from off the land whither thou goest to possess it.

64) And the Lord shall scatter thee among all people, from the one end of the earth even unto the other; and there thou shalt serve other gods, which neither thou nor thy fathers have known, even wood and stone.

65) And among these nations shalt thou find no ease, neither shall the sole of thy foot have rest: but the Lord shall give thee there a trembling heart, and failing of eyes, and sorrow of mind:

66) And thy life shall hang in doubt before thee; and thou shalt fear day and night, and shalt have none assurance of thy life:

67) In the morning thou shalt say, Would God it were even! and at even thou shalt say, Would God it were morning! for the fear of thine heart wherewith thou shalt fear, and for the sight of thine eyes which thou shalt see.

68) And the Lord shall bring thee into Egypt again with ships, by the way whereof I spake unto thee, Thou shalt see it no more again: and there ye shall be sold unto your enemies for bondmen and bondwomen, and no man shall buy you.

Deuteronomy 28:1-68

∾ 5 ∾

DAVID AND GOLIATH

1 SAMUEL 17

1) Now the Philistines gathered together their armies to battle, and were gathered together at Shochoh, which belongeth to Judah, and pitched between Shochoh and Azekah, in Ephesdammim.

2) And Saul and the men of Israel were gathered together, and pitched by the valley of Elah, and set the battle in array against the Philistines.

3) And the Philistines stood on a mountain on the one side, and Israel stood on a mountain on the other side: and there was a valley between them.

4) And there went out a champion out of the camp of the Philistines, named Goliath, of Gath, whose height was six cubits and a span.

5) And he had an helmet of brass upon his head, and he was armed with a coat of mail; and the weight of the coat was five thousand shekels of brass.

6) And he had greaves of brass upon his legs, and a target of brass between his shoulders.

7) And the staff of his spear was like a weaver's beam; and his spear's head weighed six hundred shekels of iron: and one bearing a shield

went before him.

8) And he stood and cried unto the armies of Israel, and said unto them, Why are ye come out to set your battle in array? am not I a Philistine, and ye servants to Saul? choose you a man for you, and let him come down to me.

9) If he be able to fight with me, and to kill me, then will we be your servants: but if I prevail against him, and kill him, then shall ye be our servants, and serve us.

10) And the Philistine said, I defy the armies of Israel this day; give me a man, that we may fight together.

11) When Saul and all Israel heard those words of the Philistine, they were dismayed, and greatly afraid.

12) Now David was the son of that Ephrathite of Bethlehemjudah, whose name was Jesse; and he had eight sons: and the man went among men for an old man in the days of Saul.

13) And the three eldest sons of Jesse went and followed Saul to the battle: and the names of his three sons that went to the battle were Eliab the firstborn, and next unto him Abinadab, and the third Shammah.

14) And David was the youngest: and the three eldest followed Saul.

15) But David went and returned from Saul to feed his father's sheep at Bethlehem.

16) And the Philistine drew near morning and evening, and presented himself forty days.

17) And Jesse said unto David his son, Take now for thy brethren an ephah of this parched

corn, and these ten loaves, and run to the camp to thy brethren;

18) And carry these ten cheeses unto the captain of their thousand, and look how thy brethren fare, and take their pledge.

19) Now Saul, and they, and all the men of Israel, were in the valley of Elah, fighting with the Philistines.

20) And David rose up early in the morning, and left the sheep with a keeper, and took, and went, as Jesse had commanded him; and he came to the trench, as the host was going forth to the fight, and shouted for the battle.

21) For Israel and the Philistines had put the battle in array, army against army.

22) And David left his carriage in the hand of the keeper of the carriage, and ran into the army, and came and saluted his brethren.

23) And as he talked with them, behold, there came up the champion, the Philistine of Gath, Goliath by name, out of the armies of the Philistines, and spake according to the same words: and David heard them.

24) And all the men of Israel, when they saw the man, fled from him, and were sore afraid.

25) And the men of Israel said, Have ye seen this man that is come up? surely to defy Israel is he come up: and it shall be, that the man who killeth him, the king will enrich him with great riches, and will give him his daughter, and make his father's house free in Israel.

26) And David spake to the men that stood by him, saying, What shall be done to the man that

killeth this Philistine, and taketh away the reproach from Israel? for who is this uncircumcised Philistine, that he should defy the armies of the living God?

27) And the people answered him after this manner, saying, So shall it be done to the man that killeth him.

28) And Eliab his eldest brother heard when he spake unto the men; and Eliab's anger was kindled against David, and he said, Why camest thou down hither? and with whom hast thou left those few sheep in the wilderness? I know thy pride, and the naughtiness of thine heart; for thou art come down that thou mightest see the battle.

29) And David said, What have I now done? Is there not a cause?

30) And he turned from him toward another, and spake after the same manner: and the people answered him again after the former manner.

31) And when the words were heard which David spake, they rehearsed them before Saul: and he sent for him.

32) And David said to Saul, Let no man's heart fail because of him; thy servant will go and fight with this Philistine.

33) And Saul said to David, Thou art not able to go against this Philistine to fight with him: for thou art but a youth, and he a man of war from his youth.

34) And David said unto Saul, Thy servant kept his father's sheep, and there came a lion, and a bear, and took a lamb out of the flock:

35) And I went out after him, and smote him,

and delivered it out of his mouth: and when he arose against me, I caught him by his beard, and smote him, and slew him.

36) Thy servant slew both the lion and the bear: and this uncircumcised Philistine shall be as one of them, seeing he hath defied the armies of the living God.

37) David said moreover, The Lord that delivered me out of the paw of the lion, and out of the paw of the bear, He will deliver me out of the hand of this Philistine. And Saul said unto David, Go, and the Lord be with thee.

38) And Saul armed David with his armour, and he put an helmet of brass upon his head; also he armed him with a coat of mail.

39) And David girded his sword upon his armour, and he assayed to go; for he had not proved it. And David said unto Saul, I cannot go with these; for I have not proved them. And David put them off him.

40) And he took his staff in his hand, and chose him five smooth stones out of the brook, and put them in a shepherd's bag which he had, even in a scrip; and his sling was in his hand: and he drew near to the Philistine.

41) And the Philistine came on and drew near unto David; and the man that bare the shield went before him.

42) And when the Philistine looked about, and saw David, he disdained him: for he was but a youth, and ruddy, and of a fair countenance.

43) And the Philistine said unto David, Am I a dog, that thou comest to me with staves? And the

Philistine cursed David by his gods.

44) And the Philistine said to David, Come to me, and I will give thy flesh unto the fowls of the air, and to the beasts of the field.

45) Then said David to the Philistine, Thou comest to me with a sword, and with a spear, and with a shield: but I come to thee in the name of the Lord of hosts, the God of the armies of Israel, Whom thou hast defied.

46) This day will the Lord deliver thee into mine hand; and I will smite thee, and take thine head from thee; and I will give the carcases of the host of the Philistines this day unto the fowls of the air, and to the wild beasts of the earth; that all the earth may know that there is a God in Israel.

47) And all this assembly shall know that the Lord saveth not with sword and spear: for the battle is the Lord's, and He will give you into our hands.

48) And it came to pass, when the Philistine arose, and came and drew nigh to meet David, that David hasted, and ran toward the army to meet the Philistine.

49) And David put his hand in his bag, and took thence a stone, and slang it, and smote the Philistine in his forehead, that the stone sunk into his forehead; and he fell upon his face to the earth.

50) So David prevailed over the Philistine with a sling and with a stone, and smote the Philistine, and slew him; but there was no sword in the hand of David.

51) Therefore David ran, and stood upon the Philistine, and took his sword, and drew it out of

the sheath thereof, and slew him, and cut off his head therewith. And when the Philistines saw their champion was dead, they fled.

52) And the men of Israel and of Judah arose, and shouted, and pursued the Philistines, until thou come to the valley, and to the gates of Ekron. And the wounded of the Philistines fell down by the way to Shaaraim, even unto Gath, and unto Ekron.

53) And the children of Israel returned from chasing after the Philistines, and they spoiled their tents.

54) And David took the head of the Philistine, and brought it to Jerusalem; but he put his armour in his tent.

55) And when Saul saw David go forth against the Philistine, he said unto Abner, the captain of the host, Abner, whose son is this youth? And Abner said, As thy soul liveth, O king, I cannot tell.

56) And the king said, Inquire thou whose son the stripling is.

57) And as David returned from the slaughter of the Philistine, Abner took him, and brought him before Saul with the head of the Philistine in his hand.

58) And Saul said to him, Whose son art thou, thou young man? And David answered, I am the son of thy servant Jesse the Bethlehemite.

1 Samuel 17:1-58

One Day Of Favor
Is Worth
A Thousand Days Of Labor.

-MIKE MURDOCK

6

Rewards Of
Belonging To God

PSALM 23

1) The Lord is my shepherd; I shall not want.

2) He maketh me to lie down in green pastures: He leadeth me beside the still waters.

3) He restoreth my soul: He leadeth me in the paths of righteousness for His name's sake.

4) Yea, though I walk through the valley of the shadow of death, I will fear no evil: for Thou art with me; Thy rod and Thy staff they comfort me.

5) Thou preparest a table before me in the presence of mine enemies: Thou anointest my head with oil; my cup runneth over.

6) Surely goodness and mercy shall follow me all the days of my life: and I will dwell in the house of the Lord for ever.   *Psalm 23:1-6*

What You Love Will Reward You.

-MIKE MURDOCK

≈ 7 ≈

PROTECTION

PSALM 91

1) He that dwelleth in the secret place of the most High shall abide under the shadow of the Almighty.

2) I will say of the Lord, He is my refuge and my fortress: my God; in Him will I trust.

3) Surely He shall deliver thee from the snare of the fowler, and from the noisome pestilence.

4) He shall cover thee with His feathers, and under His wings shalt thou trust: His truth shall be thy shield and buckler.

5) Thou shalt not be afraid for the terror by night; nor for the arrow that flieth by day;

6) Nor for the pestilence that walketh in darkness; nor for the destruction that wasteth at noonday.

7) A thousand shall fall at thy side, and ten thousand at thy right hand; but it shall not come nigh thee.

8) Only with thine eyes shalt thou behold and see the reward of the wicked.

9) Because thou hast made the Lord, which is my refuge, even the most High, thy habitation;

10) There shall no evil befall thee, neither shall any plague come nigh thy dwelling.

11) For He shall give His angels charge over thee, to keep thee in all thy ways.

12) They shall bear thee up in their hands, lest thou dash thy foot against a stone.

13) Thou shalt tread upon the lion and adder: the young lion and the dragon shalt thou trample under feet.

14) Because He hath set His love upon me, therefore will I deliver him: I will set him on high, because he hath known My name.

15) He shall call upon Me, and I will answer him: I will be with him in trouble; I will deliver him, and honour him.

16) With long life will I satisfy him, and shew him My salvation.   *Psalm 91:1-16*

8

THE WORD OF GOD

PSALM 119

1) Blessed are the undefiled in the way, who walk in the law of the Lord.

2) Blessed are they that keep His testimonies, and that seek Him with the whole heart.

3) They also do no iniquity: they walk in His ways.

4) Thou hast commanded us to keep Thy precepts diligently.

5) O that my ways were directed to keep Thy statutes!

6) Then shall I not be ashamed, when I have respect unto all Thy commandments.

7) I will praise thee with uprightness of heart, when I shall have learned Thy righteous judgments.

8) I will keep Thy statutes: O forsake me not utterly.

9) Wherewithal shall a young man cleanse his way? by taking heed thereto according to Thy word.

10) With my whole heart have I sought Thee: O let me not wander from Thy commandments.

11) Thy word have I hid in mine heart, that I might not sin against Thee.

12) Blessed art Thou, O Lord: teach me Thy statutes.

13) With my lips have I declared all the judgments of Thy mouth.

14) I have rejoiced in the way of Thy testimonies, as much as in all riches.

15) I will meditate in Thy precepts, and have respect unto Thy ways.

16) I will delight myself in Thy statutes: I will not forget Thy word.

17) Deal bountifully with Thy servant, that I may live, and keep Thy word.

18) Open Thou mine eyes, that I may behold wondrous things out of Thy law.

19) I am a stranger in the earth: hide not Thy commandments from me.

20) My soul breaketh for the longing that it hath unto Thy judgments at all times.

21) Thou hast rebuked the proud that are cursed, which do err from Thy commandments.

22) Remove from me reproach and contempt; for I have kept Thy testimonies.

23) Princes also did sit and speak against me: but Thy servant did meditate in Thy statutes.

24) Thy testimonies also are my delight and my counsellers.

25) My soul cleaveth unto the dust: quicken Thou me according to Thy word.

26) I have declared my ways, and Thou heardest me: teach me Thy statutes.

27) Make me to understand the way of Thy

precepts: so shall I talk of Thy wondrous works.

28) My soul melteth for heaviness: strengthen Thou me according unto Thy word.

29) Remove from me the way of lying: and grant me Thy law graciously.

30) I have chosen the way of truth: Thy judgments have I laid before me.

31) I have stuck unto Thy testimonies: O Lord, put me not to shame.

32) I will run the way of Thy commandments, when Thou shalt enlarge my heart.

33) Teach me, O Lord, the way of Thy statutes; and I shall keep it unto the end.

34) Give me understanding, and I shall keep Thy law; yea, I shall observe it with my whole heart.

35) Make me to go in the path of Thy commandments; for therein do I delight.

36) Incline my heart unto Thy testimonies, and not to covetousness.

37) Turn away mine eyes from beholding vanity; and quicken Thou me in Thy way.

38) Stablish Thy word unto Thy servant, who is devoted to Thy fear.

39) Turn away my reproach which I fear: for Thy judgments are good.

40) Behold, I have longed after Thy precepts: quicken me in Thy righteousness.

41) Let Thy mercies come also unto me, O Lord, even Thy salvation, according to Thy word.

42) So shall I have wherewith to answer him that reproacheth me: for I trust in Thy word.

43) And take not the word of truth utterly out

of my mouth; for I have hoped in Thy judgments.

44) So shall I keep Thy law continually for ever and ever.

45) And I will walk at liberty: for I seek Thy precepts.

46) I will speak of Thy testimonies also before kings, and will not be ashamed.

47) And I will delight myself in Thy commandments, which I have loved.

48) My hands also will I lift up unto Thy commandments, which I have loved; and I will meditate in Thy statutes.

49) Remember the word unto Thy servant, upon which Thou hast caused me to hope.

50) This is my comfort in my affliction: for Thy word hath quickened me.

51) The proud have had me greatly in derision: yet have I not declined from Thy law.

52) I remembered Thy judgments of old, O Lord; and have comforted myself.

53) Horror hath taken hold upon me because of the wicked that forsake Thy law.

54) Thy statutes have been my songs in the house of my pilgrimage.

55) I have remembered Thy name, O Lord, in the night, and have kept Thy law.

56) This I had, because I kept Thy precepts.

57) Thou art my portion, O Lord: I have said that I would keep Thy words.

58) I entreated Thy favour with my whole heart: be merciful unto me according to Thy word.

59) I thought on my ways, and turned my feet unto Thy testimonies.

60) I made haste, and delayed not to keep Thy commandments.

61) The bands of the wicked have robbed me: but I have not forgotten Thy law.

62) At midnight I will rise to give thanks unto Thee because of Thy righteous judgments.

63) I am a companion of all them that fear Thee, and of them that keep Thy precepts.

64) The earth, O Lord, is full of Thy mercy: teach me Thy statutes.

65) Thou hast dealt well with Thy servant, O Lord, according unto Thy word.

66) Teach me good judgment and knowledge: for I have believed Thy commandments.

67) Before I was afflicted I went astray: but now have I kept Thy word.

68) Thou art good, and doest good; teach me Thy statutes.

69) The proud have forged a lie against me: but I will keep Thy precepts with my whole heart.

70) Their heart is as fat as grease; but I delight in Thy law.

71) It is good for me that I have been afflicted; that I might learn Thy statutes.

72) The law of Thy mouth is better unto me than thousands of gold and silver.

73) Thy hands have made me and fashioned me: give me understanding, that I may learn Thy commandments.

74) They that fear Thee will be glad when they see me; because I have hoped in Thy word.

75) I know, O Lord, that Thy judgments are right, and that Thou in faithfulness hast afflicted

me.

76) Let, I pray thee, Thy merciful kindness be for my comfort, according to Thy word unto Thy servant.

77) Let Thy tender mercies come unto me, that I may live: for Thy law is my delight.

78) Let the proud be ashamed; for they dealt perversely with me without a cause: but I will meditate in Thy precepts.

79) Let those that fear Thee turn unto me, and those that have known Thy testimonies.

80) Let my heart be sound in Thy statutes; that I be not ashamed.

81) My soul fainteth for Thy salvation: but I hope in Thy word.

82) Mine eyes fail for Thy word, saying, When wilt Thou comfort me?

83) For I am become like a bottle in the smoke; yet do I not forget Thy statutes.

84) How many are the days of Thy servant? when wilt Thou execute judgment on them that persecute me?

85) The proud have digged pits for me, which are not after Thy law.

86) All Thy commandments are faithful: they persecute me wrongfully; help Thou me.

87) They had almost consumed me upon earth; but I forsook not Thy precepts.

88) Quicken me after Thy lovingkindness; so shall I keep the testimony of Thy mouth.

89) For ever, O Lord, Thy word is settled in heaven.

90) Thy faithfulness is unto all generations:

Thou hast established the earth, and it abideth.

91) They continue this day according to Thine ordinances: for all are Thy servants.

92) Unless Thy law had been my delights, I should then have perished in mine affliction.

93) I will never forget Thy precepts: for with them Thou hast quickened me.

94) I am thine, save me; for I have sought Thy precepts.

95) The wicked have waited for me to destroy me: but I will consider Thy testimonies.

96) I have seen an end of all perfection: but Thy commandment is exceeding broad.

97) O how love I Thy law! it is my meditation all the day.

98) Thou through Thy commandments hast made me wiser than mine enemies: for they are ever with me.

99) I have more understanding than all my teachers: for Thy testimonies are my meditation.

100) I understand more than the ancients, because I keep Thy precepts.

101) I have refrained my feet from every evil way, that I might keep Thy word.

102) I have not departed from Thy judgments: for Thou hast taught me.

103) How sweet are Thy words unto my taste! yea, sweeter than honey to my mouth!

104) Through Thy precepts I get understanding: therefore I hate every false way.

105) Thy word is a lamp unto my feet, and a light unto my path.

106) I have sworn, and I will perform it, that I

will keep Thy righteous judgments.

107) I am afflicted very much: quicken me, O Lord, according unto Thy word.

108) Accept, I beseech thee, the freewill offerings of my mouth, O Lord, and teach me Thy judgments.

109) My soul is continually in my hand: yet do I not forget Thy law.

110) The wicked have laid a snare for me: yet I erred not from Thy precepts.

111) Thy testimonies have I taken as an heritage for ever: for they are the rejoicing of my heart.

112) I have inclined mine heart to perform Thy statutes alway, even unto the end.

113) I hate vain thoughts: but Thy law do I love.

114) Thou art my hiding place and my shield: I hope in Thy word.

115) Depart from me, ye evildoers: for I will keep the commandments of my God.

116) Uphold me according unto Thy word, that I may live: and let me not be ashamed of my hope.

117) Hold Thou me up, and I shall be safe: and I will have respect unto Thy statutes continually.

118) Thou hast trodden down all them that err from Thy statutes: for their deceit is falsehood.

119) Thou puttest away all the wicked of the earth like dross: therefore I love Thy testimonies.

120) My flesh trembleth for fear of Thee; and I am afraid of Thy judgments.

121) I have done judgment and justice: leave

me not to mine oppressors.

122) Be surety for Thy servant for good: let not the proud oppress me.

123) Mine eyes fail for Thy salvation, and for the word of Thy righteousness.

124) Deal with Thy servant according unto Thy mercy, and teach me Thy statutes.

125) I am Thy servant; give me understanding, that I may know Thy testimonies.

126) It is time for Thee, Lord, to work: for they have made void Thy law.

127) Therefore I love Thy commandments above gold; yea, above fine gold.

128) Therefore I esteem all Thy precepts concerning all things to be right; and I hate every false way.

129) Thy testimonies are wonderful: therefore doth my soul keep them.

130) The entrance of Thy words giveth light; it giveth understanding unto the simple.

131) I opened my mouth, and panted: for I longed for Thy commandments.

132) Look Thou upon me, and be merciful unto me, as Thou usest to do unto those that love Thy name.

133) Order my steps in Thy word: and let not any iniquity have dominion over me.

134) Deliver me from the oppression of man: so will I keep Thy precepts.

135) Make Thy face to shine upon Thy servant; and teach me Thy statutes.

136) Rivers of waters run down mine eyes, because they keep not Thy law.

137) Righteous art Thou, O Lord, and upright are Thy judgments.

138) Thy testimonies that Thou hast commanded are righteous and very faithful.

139) My zeal hath consumed me, because mine enemies have forgotten Thy words.

140) Thy word is very pure: therefore Thy servant loveth it.

141) I am small and despised: yet do not I forget Thy precepts.

142) Thy righteousness is an everlasting righteousness, and Thy law is the truth.

143) Trouble and anguish have taken hold on me: yet Thy commandments are my delights.

144) The righteousness of Thy testimonies is everlasting: give me understanding, and I shall live.

145) I cried with my whole heart; hear me, O Lord: I will keep Thy statutes.

146) I cried unto Thee; save me, and I shall keep Thy testimonies.

147) I prevented the dawning of the morning, and cried: I hoped in Thy word.

148) Mine eyes prevent the night watches, that I might meditate in Thy word.

149) Hear my voice according unto Thy lovingkindness: O Lord, quicken me according to Thy judgment.

150) They draw nigh that follow after mischief: they are far from Thy law.

151) Thou art near, O Lord; and all Thy commandments are truth.

152) Concerning Thy testimonies, I have

known of old that Thou hast founded them for ever.

153) Consider mine affliction, and deliver me: for I do not forget Thy law.

154) Plead my cause, and deliver me: quicken me according to Thy word.

155) Salvation is far from the wicked: for they seek not Thy statutes.

156) Great are Thy tender mercies, O Lord: quicken me according to Thy judgments.

157) Many are my persecutors and mine enemies; yet do I not decline from Thy testimonies.

158) I beheld the transgressors, and was grieved; because they kept not Thy word.

159) Consider how I love Thy precepts: quicken me, O Lord, according to Thy loving-kindness.

160) Thy word is true from the beginning: and every one of Thy righteous judgments endureth for ever.

161) Princes have persecuted me without a cause: but my heart standeth in awe of Thy word.

162) I rejoice at Thy word, as one that findeth great spoil.

163) I hate and abhor lying: but Thy law do I love.

164) Seven times a day do I praise Thee because of Thy righteous judgments.

165) Great peace have they which love Thy law: and nothing shall offend them.

166) Lord, I have hoped for Thy salvation, and done Thy commandments.

167) My soul hath kept Thy testimonies; and I love them exceedingly.

168) I have kept Thy precepts and Thy testimonies: for all my ways are before Thee.

169) Let my cry come near before Thee, O Lord: give me understanding according to Thy word.

170) Let my supplication come before Thee: deliver me according to Thy word.

171) My lips shall utter praise, when Thou hast taught me Thy statutes.

172) My tongue shall speak of Thy word: for all Thy commandments are righteousness.

173) Let Thine hand help me; for I have chosen Thy precepts.

174) I have longed for Thy salvation, O Lord; and Thy law is my delight.

175) Let my soul live, and it shall praise Thee; and let Thy judgments help me.

176) I have gone astray like a lost sheep; seek Thy servant; for I do not forget Thy commandments. *Psalm 119:1-176*

9

WISDOM

PROVERBS 4

1) Hear, ye children, the instruction of a father, and attend to know understanding.

2) For I give you good doctrine, forsake ye not my law.

3) For I was my father's son, tender and only beloved in the sight of my mother.

4) He taught me also, and said unto me, Let thine heart retain my words: keep my commandments, and live.

5) Get wisdom, get understanding: forget it not; neither decline from the words of my mouth.

6) Forsake her not, and she shall preserve thee: love her, and she shall keep thee.

7) Wisdom is the principal thing; therefore get wisdom: and with all thy getting get understanding.

8) Exalt her, and she shall promote thee: she shall bring thee to honour, when thou dost embrace her.

9) She shall give to thine head an ornament of grace: a crown of glory shall she deliver to thee.

10) Hear, O my son, and receive my sayings; and the years of thy life shall be many.

11) I have taught thee in the way of wisdom; I have led thee in right paths.

12) When thou goest, thy steps shall not be straitened; and when thou runnest, thou shalt not stumble.

13) Take fast hold of instruction; let her not go: keep her; for she is thy life.

14) Enter not into the path of the wicked, and go not in the way of evil men.

15) Avoid it, pass not by it, turn from it, and pass away.

16) For they sleep not, except they have done mischief; and their sleep is taken away, unless they cause some to fall.

17) For they eat the bread of wickedness, and drink the wine of violence.

18) But the path of the just is as the shining light, that shineth more and more unto the perfect day.

19) The way of the wicked is as darkness: they know not at what they stumble.

20) My son, attend to my words; incline thine ear unto my sayings.

21) Let them not depart from thine eyes; keep them in the midst of thine heart.

22) For they are life unto those that find them, and health to all their flesh.

23) Keep thy heart with all diligence; for out of it are the issues of life.

24) Put away from thee a froward mouth, and perverse lips put far from thee.

25) Let thine eyes look right on, and let thine eyelids look straight before thee.

26) Ponder the path of thy feet, and let all thy ways be established.

27) Turn not to the right hand nor to the left: remove thy foot from evil.   *Proverbs 4:1-27*

❧ 10 ❧

THE HIGHEST QUALITY
OF WOMAN KNOWN

PROVERBS 31

1) The words of king Lemuel, the prophecy that his mother taught him.

2) What, my son? and what, the son of my womb? and what, the son of my vows?

3) Give not thy strength unto women, nor thy ways to that which destroyeth kings.

4) It is not for kings, O Lemuel, it is not for kings to drink wine; nor for princes strong drink:

5) Lest they drink, and forget the law, and pervert the judgment of any of the afflicted.

6) Give strong drink unto him that is ready to perish, and wine unto those that be of heavy hearts.

7) Let him drink, and forget his poverty, and remember his misery no more.

8) Open thy mouth for the dumb in the cause of all such as are appointed to destruction.

9) Open thy mouth, judge righteously, and plead the cause of the poor and needy.

10) Who can find a virtuous woman? for her price is far above rubies.

11) The heart of her husband doth safely trust in her, so that he shall have no need of spoil.

12) She will do him good and not evil all the days of her life.

13) She seeketh wool, and flax, and worketh willingly with her hands.

14) She is like the merchants' ships; she bringeth her food from afar.

15) She riseth also while it is yet night, and giveth meat to her household, and a portion to her maidens.

16) She considereth a field, and buyeth it: with the fruit of her hands she planteth a vineyard.

17) She girdeth her loins with strength, and strengtheneth her arms.

18) She perceiveth that her merchandise is good: her candle goeth not out by night.

19) She layeth her hands to the spindle, and her hands hold the distaff.

20) She stretcheth out her hand to the poor; yea, she reacheth forth her hands to the needy.

21) She is not afraid of the snow for her household: for all her household are clothed with scarlet.

22) She maketh herself coverings of tapestry; her clothing is silk and purple.

23) Her husband is known in the gates, when he sitteth among the elders of the land.

24) She maketh fine linen, and selleth it; and delivereth girdles unto the merchant.

25) Strength and honour are her clothing; and she shall rejoice in time to come.

26) She openeth her mouth with wisdom; and

in her tongue is the law of kindness.

27) She looketh well to the ways of her household, and eateth not the bread of idleness.

28) Her children arise up, and call her blessed; her husband also, and he praiseth her.

29) Many daughters have done virtuously, but thou excellest them all.

30) Favour is deceitful, and beauty is vain: but a woman that feareth the Lord, she shall be praised.

31) Give her of the fruit of her hands; and let her own works praise her in the gates.

Proverbs 31:1-31

Warfare Always Surrounds The Birth Of A Miracle.

-MIKE MURDOCK

🙠 11 🙠

BIRTH OF JESUS

MATTHEW 1

1) The book of the generation of Jesus Christ, the son of David, the son of Abraham.

2) Abraham begat Isaac; and Isaac begat Jacob; and Jacob begat Judas and his brethren;

3) And Judas begat Phares and Zara of Thamar; and Phares begat Esrom; and Esrom begat Aram;

4) And Aram begat Aminadab; and Aminadab begat Naasson; and Naasson begat Salmon;

5) And Salmon begat Booz of Rachab; and Booz begat Obed of Ruth; and Obed begat Jesse;

6) And Jesse begat David the king; and David the king begat Solomon of her that had been the wife of Urias;

7) And Solomon begat Roboam; and Roboam begat Abia; and Abia begat Asa;

8) And Asa begat Josaphat; and Josaphat begat Joram; and Joram begat Ozias;

9) And Ozias begat Joatham; and Joatham begat Achaz; and Achaz begat Ezekias;

10) And Ezekias begat Manasses; and Manasses begat Amon; and Amon begat Josias;

11) And Josias begat Jechonias and his brethren, about the time they were carried away to

Babylon:

12) And after they were brought to Babylon, Jechonias begat Salathiel; and Salathiel begat Zorobabel;

13) And Zorobabel begat Abiud; and Abiud begat Eliakim; and Eliakim begat Azor;

14) And Azor begat Sadoc; and Sadoc begat Achim; and Achim begat Eliud;

15) And Eliud begat Eleazar; and Eleazar begat Matthan; and Matthan begat Jacob;

16) And Jacob begat Joseph the husband of Mary, of whom was born Jesus, Who is called Christ.

17) So all the generations from Abraham to David are fourteen generations; and from David until the carrying away into Babylon are fourteen generations; and from the carrying away into Babylon unto Christ are fourteen generations.

18) Now the birth of Jesus Christ was on this wise: When as His mother Mary was espoused to Joseph, before they came together, she was found with child of the Holy Ghost.

19) Then Joseph her husband, being a just man, and not willing to make her a public example, was minded to put her away privily.

20) But while he thought on these things, behold, the angel of the Lord appeared unto him in a dream, saying, Joseph, thou son of David, fear not to take unto thee Mary thy wife: for that which is conceived in her is of the Holy Ghost.

21) And she shall bring forth a son, and thou shalt call His name Jesus: for He shall save His people from their sins.

22) Now all this was done, that it might be

fulfilled which was spoken of the Lord by the prophet, saying,

23) Behold, a virgin shall be with child, and shall bring forth a son, and they shall call His name Emmanuel, which being interpreted is, God with us.

24) Then Joseph being raised from sleep did as the angel of the Lord had bidden him, and took unto him his wife:

25) And knew her not till she had brought forth her firstborn son: and he called His name Jesus. *Matthew 1:1-25*

What You Are Willing To Walk Away From Determines What God Will Bring To You.

-MIKE MURDOCK

～ 12 ～

TEMPTATIONS OF JESUS

MATTHEW 4

1) Then was Jesus led up of the Spirit into the wilderness to be tempted of the devil.

2) And when He had fasted forty days and forty nights, He was afterward an hungred.

3) And when the tempter came to Him, he said, If Thou be the Son of God, command that these stones be made bread.

4) But He answered and said, It is written, Man shall not live by bread alone, but by every word that proceedeth out of the mouth of God.

5) Then the devil taketh Him up into the holy city, and setteth Him on a pinnacle of the temple,

6) And saith unto Him, If Thou be the Son of God, cast Thyself down: for it is written, He shall give His angels charge concerning Thee: and in their hands they shall bear Thee up, lest at any time Thou dash Thy foot against a stone.

7) Jesus said unto him, It is written again, Thou shalt not tempt the Lord thy God.

8) Again, the devil taketh Him up into an exceeding high mountain, and sheweth Him all the kingdoms of the world, and the glory of them;

9) And saith unto Him, All these things will I give Thee, if Thou wilt fall down and worship me.

10) Then saith Jesus unto him, Get thee hence, satan: for it is written, Thou shalt worship the Lord thy God, and Him only shalt thou serve.

11) Then the devil leaveth Him, and, behold, angels came and ministered unto Him.

12) Now when Jesus had heard that John was cast into prison, He departed into Galilee;

13) And leaving Nazareth, He came and dwelt in Capernaum, which is upon the sea coast, in the borders of Zabulon and Nephthalim:

14) That it might be fulfilled which was spoken by Esaias the prophet, saying,

15) The land of Zabulon, and the land of Nephthalim, by the way of the sea, beyond Jordan, Galilee of the Gentiles;

16) The people which sat in darkness saw great light; and to them which sat in the region and shadow of death light is sprung up.

17) From that time Jesus began to preach, and to say, Repent: for the kingdom of heaven is at hand.

18) And Jesus, walking by the sea of Galilee, saw two brethren, Simon called Peter, and Andrew his brother, casting a net into the sea: for they were fishers.

19) And He saith unto them, Follow Me, and I will make you fishers of men.

20) And they straightway left their nets, and followed Him.

21) And going on from thence, He saw other two brethren, James the son of Zebedee, and John

his brother, in a ship with Zebedee their father, mending their nets; and He called them.

22) And they immediately left the ship and their father, and followed Him.

23) And Jesus went about all Galilee, teaching in their synagogues, and preaching the gospel of the kingdom, and healing all manner of sickness and all manner of disease among the people.

24) And His fame went throughout all Syria: and they brought unto Him all sick people that were taken with divers diseases and torments, and those which were possessed with devils, and those which were lunatic, and those that had the palsy; and He healed them.

25) And there followed Him great multitudes of people from Galilee, and from Decapolis, and from Jerusalem, and from Judaea, and from beyond Jordan. *Matthew 4:1-25*

Your Rewards In Life
Are Determined
By The Kinds Of Problems
You Are Willing To Solve
For Others.

-MIKE MURDOCK

⟿ 13 ⟿

BEATITUDES

MATTHEW 5

1) And seeing the multitudes, He went up into a mountain: and when He was set, His disciples came unto Him:

2) And He opened His mouth, and taught them, saying,

3) Blessed are the poor in spirit: for theirs is the kingdom of heaven.

4) Blessed are they that mourn: for they shall be comforted.

5) Blessed are the meek: for they shall inherit the earth.

6) Blessed are they which do hunger and thirst after righteousness: for they shall be filled.

7) Blessed are the merciful: for they shall obtain mercy.

8) Blessed are the pure in heart: for they shall see God.

9) Blessed are the peacemakers: for they shall be called the children of God.

10) Blessed are they which are persecuted for righteousness' sake: for theirs is the kingdom of heaven.

11) Blessed are ye, when men shall revile you,

and persecute you, and shall say all manner of evil against you falsely, for My sake.

12) Rejoice, and be exceeding glad: for great is your reward in heaven: for so persecuted they the prophets which were before you.

13) Ye are the salt of the earth: but if the salt have lost his savour, wherewith shall it be salted? it is thenceforth good for nothing, but to be cast out, and to be trodden under foot of men.

14) Ye are the light of the world. A city that is set on an hill cannot be hid.

15) Neither do men light a candle, and put it under a bushel, but on a candlestick; and it giveth light unto all that are in the house.

16) Let your light so shine before men, that they may see your good works, and glorify your Father which is in heaven.

17) Think not that I am come to destroy the law, or the prophets: I am not come to destroy, but to fulfil.

18) For verily I say unto you, Till heaven and earth pass, one jot or one tittle shall in no wise pass from the law, till all be fulfilled.

19) Whosoever therefore shall break one of these least commandments, and shall teach men so, he shall be called the least in the kingdom of heaven: but whosoever shall do and teach them, the same shall be called great in the kingdom of heaven.

20) For I say unto you, That except your righteousness shall exceed the righteousness of the scribes and Pharisees, ye shall in no case enter into the kingdom of heaven.

21) Ye have heard that it was said by them of old time, Thou shalt not kill; and whosoever shall kill shall be in danger of the judgment:

22) But I say unto you, That whosoever is angry with his brother without a cause shall be in danger of the judgment: and whosoever shall say to his brother, Raca, shall be in danger of the council: but whosoever shall say, Thou fool, shall be in danger of hell fire.

23) Therefore if thou bring thy gift to the altar, and there rememberest that thy brother hath aught against thee;

24) Leave there thy gift before the altar, and go thy way; first be reconciled to thy brother, and then come and offer thy gift.

25) Agree with thine adversary quickly, whiles thou art in the way with him; lest at any time the adversary deliver thee to the judge, and the judge deliver thee to the officer, and thou be cast into prison.

26) Verily I say unto thee, Thou shalt by no means come out thence, till thou hast paid the uttermost farthing.

27) Ye have heard that it was said by them of old time, Thou shalt not commit adultery:

28) But I say unto you, That whosoever looketh on a woman to lust after her hath committed adultery with her already in his heart.

29) And if thy right eye offend thee, pluck it out, and cast it from thee: for it is profitable for thee that one of thy members should perish, and not that thy whole body should be cast into hell.

30) And if thy right hand offend thee, cut it

off, and cast it from thee: for it is profitable for thee that one of thy members should perish, and not that thy whole body should be cast into hell.

31) It hath been said, Whosoever shall put away his wife, let him give her a writing of divorcement:

32) But I say unto you, That whosoever shall put away his wife, saving for the cause of fornication, causeth her to commit adultery: and whosoever shall marry her that is divorced committeth adultery.

33) Again, ye have heard that it hath been said by them of old time, Thou shalt not forswear thyself, but shalt perform unto the Lord thine oaths:

34) But I say unto you, Swear not at all; neither by heaven; for it is God's throne:

35) Nor by the earth; for it is His footstool: neither by Jerusalem; for it is the city of the great King.

36) Neither shalt thou swear by thy head, because thou canst not make one hair white or black.

37) But let your communication be, Yea, yea; Nay, nay: for whatsoever is more than these cometh of evil.

38) Ye have heard that it hath been said, An eye for an eye, and a tooth for a tooth:

39) But I say unto you, That ye resist not evil: but whosoever shall smite thee on thy right cheek, turn to him the other also.

40) And if any man will sue thee at the law, and take away thy coat, let him have thy cloak also.

41) And whosoever shall compel thee to go a mile, go with him twain.

42) Give to him that asketh thee, and from him that would borrow of thee turn not thou away.

43) Ye have heard that it hath been said, Thou shalt love thy neighbour, and hate thine enemy.

44) But I say unto you, Love your enemies, bless them that curse you, do good to them that hate you, and pray for them which despitefully use you, and persecute you;

45) That ye may be the children of your Father which is in heaven: for He maketh His sun to rise on the evil and on the good, and sendeth rain on the just and on the unjust.

46) For if ye love them which love you, what reward have ye? do not even the publicans the same?

47) And if ye salute your brethren only, what do ye more than others? do not even the publicans so?

48) Be ye therefore perfect, even as your Father which is in heaven is perfect.

Matthew 5:1-48

What You Make Happen
For Others
God Will Make Happen
For You.

-MIKE MURDOCK

❧ **14** ❧

THE GOLDEN RULE

━━━━━━◦❖◦━━━━━━

MATTHEW 7

1) Judge not, that ye be not judged.

2) For with what judgment ye judge, ye shall be judged: and with what measure ye mete, it shall be measured to you again.

3) And why beholdest thou the mote that is in thy brother's eye, but considerest not the beam that is in thine own eye?

4) Or how wilt thou say to thy brother, Let me pull out the mote out of thine eye; and, behold, a beam is in thine own eye?

5) Thou hypocrite, first cast out the beam out of thine own eye; and then shalt thou see clearly to cast out the mote out of thy brother's eye.

6) Give not that which is holy unto the dogs, neither cast ye your pearls before swine, lest they trample them under their feet, and turn again and rend you.

7) Ask, and it shall be given you; seek, and ye shall find; knock, and it shall be opened unto you:

8) For every one that asketh receiveth; and he that seeketh findeth; and to him that knocketh it shall be opened.

9) Or what man is there of you, whom if his

son ask bread, will he give him a stone?

10) Or if he ask a fish, will he give him a serpent?

11) If ye then, being evil, know how to give good gifts unto your children, how much more shall your Father which is in heaven give good things to them that ask Him?

12) Therefore all things whatsoever ye would that men should do to you, do ye even so to them: for this is the law and the prophets.

13) Enter ye in at the strait gate: for wide is the gate, and broad is the way, that leadeth to destruction, and many there be which go in thereat:

14) Because strait is the gate, and narrow is the way, which leadeth unto life, and few there be that find it.

15) Beware of false prophets, which come to you in sheep's clothing, but inwardly they are ravening wolves.

16) Ye shall know them by their fruits. Do men gather grapes of thorns, or figs of thistles?

17) Even so every good tree bringeth forth good fruit; but a corrupt tree bringeth forth evil fruit.

18) A good tree cannot bring forth evil fruit, neither can a corrupt tree bring forth good fruit.

19) Every tree that bringeth not forth good fruit is hewn down, and cast into the fire.

20) Wherefore by their fruits ye shall know them.

21) Not every one that saith unto me, Lord, Lord, shall enter into the kingdom of heaven; but

he that doeth the will of My Father which is in heaven.

22) Many will say to Me in that day, Lord, Lord, have we not prophesied in Thy name? and in Thy name have cast out devils? and in Thy name done many wonderful works?

23) And then will I profess unto them, I never knew you: depart from Me, ye that work iniquity.

24) Therefore whosoever heareth these sayings of Mine, and doeth them, I will liken him unto a wise man, which built his house upon a rock:

25) And the rain descended, and the floods came, and the winds blew, and beat upon that house; and it fell not: for it was founded upon a rock.

26) And every one that heareth these sayings of Mine, and doeth them not, shall be likened unto a foolish man, which built his house upon the sand:

27) And the rain descended, and the floods came, and the winds blew, and beat upon that house; and it fell: and great was the fall of it.

28) And it came to pass, when Jesus had ended these sayings, the people were astonished at His doctrine:

29) For He taught them as one having authority, and not as the scribes.

Matthew 7:1-29

God Never Responds
To Pain,
God Always Responds
To Pursuit.

-MIKE MURDOCK

～ 15 ～

The Healing And Miracle Power Of Jesus

Matthew 14

1) At that time Herod the tetrarch heard of the fame of Jesus,

2) And said unto his servants, This is John the Baptist; he is risen from the dead; and therefore mighty works do shew forth themselves in him.

3) For Herod had laid hold on John, and bound him, and put him in prison for Herodias' sake, his brother Philip's wife.

4) For John said unto him, It is not lawful for thee to have her.

5) And when he would have put him to death, he feared the multitude, because they counted him as a prophet.

6) But when Herod's birthday was kept, the daughter of Herodias danced before them, and pleased Herod.

7) Whereupon he promised with an oath to give her whatsoever she would ask.

8) And she, being before instructed of her mother, said, Give me here John Baptist's head in a charger.

9) And the king was sorry: nevertheless for the oath's sake, and them which sat with him at meat, he commanded it to be given her.

10) And he sent, and beheaded John in the prison.

11) And his head was brought in a charger, and given to the damsel: and she brought it to her mother.

12) And his disciples came, and took up the body, and buried it, and went and told Jesus.

13) When Jesus heard of it, He departed thence by ship into a desert place apart: and when the people had heard thereof, they followed Him on foot out of the cities.

14) And Jesus went forth, and saw a great multitude, and was moved with compassion toward them, and He healed their sick.

15) And when it was evening, His disciples came to Him, saying, This is a desert place, and the time is now past; send the multitude away, that they may go into the villages, and buy themselves victuals.

16) But Jesus said unto them, They need not depart; give ye them to eat.

17) And they say unto Him, We have here but five loaves, and two fishes.

18) He said, Bring them hither to Me.

19) And He commanded the multitude to sit down on the grass, and took the five loaves, and the two fishes, and looking up to heaven, He blessed, and brake, and gave the loaves to His disciples, and

the disciples to the multitude.

20) And they did all eat, and were filled: and they took up of the fragments that remained twelve baskets full.

21) And they that had eaten were about five thousand men, beside women and children.

22) And straightway Jesus constrained His disciples to get into a ship, and to go before Him unto the other side, while He sent the multitudes away.

23) And when He had sent the multitudes away, He went up into a mountain apart to pray: and when the evening was come, He was there alone.

24) But the ship was now in the midst of the sea, tossed with waves: for the wind was contrary.

25) And in the fourth watch of the night Jesus went unto them, walking on the sea.

26) And when the disciples saw Him walking on the sea, they were troubled, saying, It is a spirit; and they cried out for fear.

27) But straightway Jesus spake unto them, saying, Be of good cheer; it is I; be not afraid.

28) And Peter answered Him and said, Lord, if it be Thou, bid me come unto Thee on the water.

29) And He said, Come. And when Peter was come down out of the ship, he walked on the water, to go to Jesus.

30) But when he saw the wind boisterous, he was afraid; and beginning to sink, he cried, saying, Lord, save me.

31) And immediately Jesus stretched forth His hand, and caught him, and said unto him, O thou of little faith, wherefore didst thou doubt?

32) And when they were come into the ship, the wind ceased.

33) Then they that were in the ship came and worshipped Him, saying, Of a truth Thou art the Son of God.

34) And when they were gone over, they came into the land of Gennesaret.

35) And when the men of that place had knowledge of Him, they sent out into all that country round about, and brought unto Him all that were diseased;

36) And besought Him that they might only touch the hem of His garment: and as many as touched were made perfectly whole.

Matthew 14:1-36

∾ 16 ∾
THE CRUCIFIXION
OF JESUS

MATTHEW 27

1) When the morning was come, all the chief priests and elders of the people took counsel against Jesus to put Him to death:

2) And when they had bound Him, they led Him away, and delivered Him to Pontius Pilate the governor.

3) Then Judas, which had betrayed Him, when he saw that He was condemned, repented himself, and brought again the thirty pieces of silver to the chief priests and elders,

4) Saying, I have sinned in that I have betrayed the innocent blood. And they said, What is that to us? see thou to that.

5) And he cast down the pieces of silver in the temple, and departed, and went and hanged himself.

6) And the chief priests took the silver pieces, and said, It is not lawful for to put them into the treasury, because it is the price of blood.

7) And they took counsel, and bought with them the potter's field, to bury strangers in.

8) Wherefore that field was called, The field

of blood, unto this day.

9) Then was fulfilled that which was spoken by Jeremy the prophet, saying, And they took the thirty pieces of silver, the price of Him that was valued, whom they of the children of Israel did value;

10) And gave them for the potter's field, as the Lord appointed me.

11) And Jesus stood before the governor: and the governor asked Him, saying, Art Thou the King of the Jews? And Jesus said unto him, Thou sayest.

12) And when He was accused of the chief priests and elders, He answered nothing.

13) Then said Pilate unto Him, Hearest Thou not how many things they witness against Thee?

14) And He answered him to never a word; insomuch that the governor marvelled greatly.

15) Now at that feast the governor was wont to release unto the people a prisoner, whom they would.

16) And they had then a notable prisoner, called Barabbas.

17) Therefore when they were gathered together, Pilate said unto them, Whom will ye that I release unto you? Barabbas, or Jesus which is called Christ?

18) For he knew that for envy they had delivered him.

19) When he was set down on the judgment seat, his wife sent unto him, saying, Have thou nothing to do with that just man: for I have suffered many things this day in a dream because of Him.

20) But the chief priests and elders persuaded the multitude that they should ask Barabbas, and destroy Jesus.

21) The governor answered and said unto them, Whether of the twain will ye that I release unto you? They said, Barabbas.

22) Pilate saith unto them, What shall I do then with Jesus which is called Christ? They all say unto him, Let Him be crucified.

23) And the governor said, Why, what evil hath He done? But they cried out the more, saying, Let Him be crucified.

24) When Pilate saw that he could prevail nothing, but that rather a tumult was made, he took water, and washed his hands before the multitude, saying, I am innocent of the blood of this just person: see ye to it.

25) Then answered all the people, and said, His blood be on us, and on our children.

26) Then released he Barabbas unto them: and when he had scourged Jesus, he delivered Him to be crucified.

27) Then the soldiers of the governor took Jesus into the common hall, and gathered unto Him the whole band of soldiers.

28) And they stripped Him, and put on Him a scarlet robe.

29) And when they had platted a crown of thorns, they put it upon His head, and a reed in His right hand: and they bowed the knee before Him, and mocked Him, saying, Hail, King of the Jews!

30) And they spit upon Him, and took the reed, and smote Him on the head.

31) And after that they had mocked Him, they

took the robe off from Him, and put His own raiment on Him, and led Him away to crucify Him.

32) And as they came out, they found a man of Cyrene, Simon by name: him they compelled to bear His cross.

33) And when they were come unto a place called Golgotha, that is to say, a place of a skull,

34) They gave Him vinegar to drink mingled with gall: and when He had tasted thereof, He would not drink.

35) And they crucified Him, and parted His garments, casting lots: that it might be fulfilled which was spoken by the prophet, They parted My garments among them, and upon My vesture did they cast lots.

36) And sitting down they watched Him there;

37) And set up over His head His accusation written, THIS IS JESUS THE KING OF THE JEWS.

38) Then were there two thieves crucified with Him, one on the right hand, and another on the left.

39) And they that passed by reviled Him, wagging their heads,

40) And saying, Thou that destroyest the temple, and buildest it in three days, save Thyself. If Thou be the Son of God, come down from the cross.

41) Likewise also the chief priests mocking Him, with the scribes and elders, said,

42) He saved others; Himself He cannot save. If He be the King of Israel, let Him now come down from the cross, and we will believe Him.

43) He trusted in God; let Him deliver Him

now, if He will have Him: for He said, I am the Son of God.

44) The thieves also, which were crucified with Him, cast the same in His teeth.

45) Now from the sixth hour there was darkness over all the land unto the ninth hour.

46) And about the ninth hour Jesus cried with a loud voice, saying, Eli, Eli, lama sabachthani? that is to say, My God, My God, why hast Thou forsaken Me?

47) Some of them that stood there, when they heard that, said, This man calleth for Elias.

48) And straightway one of them ran, and took a sponge, and filled it with vinegar, and put it on a reed, and gave Him to drink.

49) The rest said, Let be, let us see whether Elias will come to save Him.

50) Jesus, when He had cried again with a loud voice, yielded up the ghost.

51) And, behold, the veil of the temple was rent in twain from the top to the bottom; and the earth did quake, and the rocks rent;

52) And the graves were opened; and many bodies of the saints which slept arose,

53) And came out of the graves after His resurrection, and went into the holy city, and appeared unto many.

54) Now when the centurion, and they that were with him, watching Jesus, saw the earthquake, and those things that were done, they feared greatly, saying, Truly this was the Son of God.

55) And many women were there beholding afar off, which followed Jesus from Galilee,

ministering unto Him:

56) Among which was Mary Magdalene, and Mary the mother of James and Joses, and the mother of Zebedee's children.

57) When the even was come, there came a rich man of Arimathaea, named Joseph, who also himself was Jesus' disciple:

58) He went to Pilate, and begged the body of Jesus. Then Pilate commanded the body to be delivered.

59) And when Joseph had taken the body, he wrapped it in a clean linen cloth,

60) And laid it in his own new tomb, which he had hewn out in the rock: and he rolled a great stone to the door of the sepulchre, and departed.

61) And there was Mary Magdalene, and the other Mary, sitting over against the sepulchre.

62) Now the next day, that followed the day of the preparation, the chief priests and Pharisees came together unto Pilate,

63) Saying, Sir, we remember that that deceiver said, while He was yet alive, After three days I will rise again.

64) Command therefore that the sepulchre be made sure until the third day, lest His disciples come by night, and steal Him away, and say unto the people, He is risen from the dead: so the last error shall be worse than the first.

65) Pilate said unto them, Ye have a watch: go your way, make it as sure as ye can.

66) So they went, and made the sepulchre sure, sealing the stone, and setting a watch.

Matthew 27:1-66

❧ 17 ❧

THE GREATEST COMMANDMENT

MARK 12

1) And He began to speak unto them by parables. A certain man planted a vineyard, and set an hedge about it, and digged a place for the winevat, and built a tower, and let it out to husbandmen, and went into a far country.

2) And at the season he sent to the husbandmen a servant, that he might receive from the husbandmen of the fruit of the vineyard.

3) And they caught him, and beat him, and sent him away empty.

4) And again he sent unto them another servant; and at him they cast stones, and wounded him in the head, and sent him away shamefully handled.

5) And again he sent another; and him they killed, and many others; beating some, and killing some.

6) Having yet therefore one son, his wellbeloved, he sent him also last unto them, saying, They will reverence my son.

7) But those husbandmen said among themselves, This is the heir; come, let us kill him,

and the inheritance shall be ours.

8) And they took him, and killed him, and cast him out of the vineyard.

9) What shall therefore the lord of the vineyard do? he will come and destroy the husbandmen, and will give the vineyard unto others.

10) And have ye not read this scripture; The stone which the builders rejected is become the head of the corner:

11) This was the Lord's doing, and it is marvellous in our eyes?

12) And they sought to lay hold on Him, but feared the people: for they knew that He had spoken the parable against them: and they left Him, and went their way.

13) And they send unto Him certain of the Pharisees and of the Herodians, to catch Him in His words.

14) And when they were come, they say unto Him, Master, we know that Thou art true, and carest for no man: for Thou regardest not the person of men, but teachest the way of God in truth: Is it lawful to give tribute to Caesar, or not?

15) Shall we give, or shall we not give? But He, knowing their hypocrisy, said unto them, Why tempt ye Me? bring Me a penny, that I may see it.

16) And they brought it. And He saith unto them, Whose is this image and superscription? And they said unto Him, Caesar's.

17) And Jesus answering said unto them, Render to Caesar the things that are Caesar's, and to God the things that are God's. And they marvelled at Him.

18) Then come unto Him the Sadducees,

which say there is no resurrection; and they asked Him, saying,

19) Master, Moses wrote unto us, If a man's brother die, and leave his wife behind him, and leave no children, that his brother should take his wife, and raise up seed unto his brother.

20) Now there were seven brethren: and the first took a wife, and dying left no seed.

21) And the second took her, and died, neither left he any seed: and the third likewise.

22) And the seven had her, and left no seed: last of all the woman died also.

23) In the resurrection therefore, when they shall rise, whose wife shall she be of them? for the seven had her to wife.

24) And Jesus answering said unto them, Do ye not therefore err, because ye know not the scriptures, neither the power of God?

25) For when they shall rise from the dead, they neither marry, nor are given in marriage; but are as the angels which are in heaven.

26) And as touching the dead, that they rise: have ye not read in the book of Moses, how in the bush God spake unto him, saying, I am the God of Abraham, and the God of Isaac, and the God of Jacob?

27) He is not the God of the dead, but the God of the living: ye therefore do greatly err.

28) And one of the scribes came, and having heard them reasoning together, and perceiving that He had answered them well, asked Him, Which is the first commandment of all?

29) And Jesus answered him, The first of all the commandments is, Hear, O Israel; The Lord our God is one Lord:

30) And thou shalt love the Lord thy God with all thy heart, and with all thy soul, and with all thy mind, and with all thy strength: this is the first commandment.

31) And the second is like, namely this, Thou shalt love thy neighbour as thyself. There is none other commandment greater than these.

32) And the scribe said unto Him, Well, Master, Thou hast said the truth: for there is one God; and there is none other but He:

33) And to love Him with all the heart, and with all the understanding, and with all the soul, and with all the strength, and to love his neighbour as himself, is more than all whole burnt offerings and sacrifices.

34) And when Jesus saw that he answered discreetly, He said unto him, Thou art not far from the kingdom of God. And no man after that durst ask Him any question.

35) And Jesus answered and said, while He taught in the temple, How say the scribes that Christ is the son of David?

36) For David himself said by the Holy Ghost, The Lord said to my Lord, Sit thou on My right hand, till I make thine enemies thy footstool.

37) David therefore himself calleth Him Lord; and whence is he then His son? And the common people heard Him gladly.

38) And He said unto them in His doctrine, Beware of the scribes, which love to go in long clothing, and love salutations in the marketplaces,

39) And the chief seats in the synagogues, and the uppermost rooms at feasts:

40) Which devour widows' houses, and for a

pretence make long prayers: these shall receive greater damnation.

41) And Jesus sat over against the treasury, and beheld how the people cast money into the treasury: and many that were rich cast in much.

42) And there came a certain poor widow, and she threw in two mites, which make a farthing.

43) And He called unto Him his disciples, and saith unto them, Verily I say unto you, That this poor widow hath cast more in, than all they which have cast into the treasury:

44) For all they did cast in of their abundance; but she of her want did cast in all that she had, even all her living.   *Mark 12:1-44*

The Proof Of Love
Is The
Investment Of Time.

-MIKE MURDOCK

≈ 18 ≈

RESURRECTION OF JESUS

MARK 16

1) And when the sabbath was past, Mary Magdalene, and Mary the mother of James, and Salome, had bought sweet spices, that they might come and anoint Him.

2) And very early in the morning the first day of the week, they came unto the sepulchre at the rising of the sun.

3) And they said among themselves, Who shall roll us away the stone from the door of the sepulchre?

4) And when they looked, they saw that the stone was rolled away: for it was very great.

5) And entering into the sepulchre, they saw a young man sitting on the right side, clothed in a long white garment; and they were affrighted.

6) And he saith unto them, Be not affrighted: Ye seek Jesus of Nazareth, Which was crucified: He is risen; He is not here: behold the place where they laid Him.

7) But go your way, tell His disciples and Peter that He goeth before you into Galilee: there shall ye see Him, as He said unto you.

8) And they went out quickly, and fled from the sepulchre; for they trembled and were amazed: neither said they any thing to any man; for they

were afraid.

9) Now when Jesus was risen early the first day of the week, He appeared first to Mary Magdalene, out of whom He had cast seven devils.

10) And she went and told them that had been with Him, as they mourned and wept.

11) And they, when they had heard that He was alive, and had been seen of her, believed not.

12) After that He appeared in another form unto two of them, as they walked, and went into the country.

13) And they went and told it unto the residue: neither believed they them.

14) Afterward He appeared unto the eleven as they sat at meat, and upbraided them with their unbelief and hardness of heart, because they believed not them which had seen Him after He was risen.

15) And He said unto them, Go ye into all the world, and preach the gospel to every creature.

16) He that believeth and is baptized shall be saved; but he that believeth not shall be damned.

17) And these signs shall follow them that believe; In My name shall they cast out devils; they shall speak with new tongues;

18) They shall take up serpents; and if they drink any deadly thing, it shall not hurt them; they shall lay hands on the sick, and they shall recover.

19) So then after the Lord had spoken unto them, He was received up into heaven, and sat on the right hand of God.

20) And they went forth, and preached every where, the Lord working with them, and confirming the word with signs following. Amen.

Mark 16:1-20

❧ **19** ❧

THE PRODIGAL SON

➤━➂━◉━◅━

LUKE 15

1) Then drew near unto Him all the publicans and sinners for to hear Him.

2) And the Pharisees and scribes murmured, saying, This man receiveth sinners, and eateth with them.

3) And He spake this parable unto them, saying,

4) What man of you, having an hundred sheep, if he lose one of them, doth not leave the ninety and nine in the wilderness, and go after that which is lost, until he find it?

5) And when he hath found it, he layeth it on his shoulders, rejoicing.

6) And when he cometh home, he calleth together his friends and neighbours, saying unto them, Rejoice with me; for I have found my sheep which was lost.

7) I say unto you, that likewise joy shall be in heaven over one sinner that repenteth, more than over ninety and nine just persons, which need no repentance.

8) Either what woman having ten pieces of silver, if she lose one piece, doth not light a candle,

and sweep the house, and seek diligently till she find it?

9) And when she hath found it, she calleth her friends and her neighbours together, saying, Rejoice with me; for I have found the piece which I had lost.

10) Likewise, I say unto you, there is joy in the presence of the angels of God over one sinner that repenteth.

11) And He said, A certain man had two sons:

12) And the younger of them said to his father, Father, give me the portion of goods that falleth to me. And he divided unto them his living.

13) And not many days after the younger son gathered all together, and took his journey into a far country, and there wasted his substance with riotous living.

14) And when he had spent all, there arose a mighty famine in that land; and he began to be in want.

15) And he went and joined himself to a citizen of that country; and he sent him into his fields to feed swine.

16) And he would fain have filled his belly with the husks that the swine did eat: and no man gave unto him.

17) And when he came to himself, he said, How many hired servants of my father's have bread enough and to spare, and I perish with hunger!

18) I will arise and go to my father, and will say unto him, Father, I have sinned against heaven, and before thee,

19) And am no more worthy to be called thy son: make me as one of thy hired servants.

20) And he arose, and came to his father. But when he was yet a great way off, his father saw him, and had compassion, and ran, and fell on his neck, and kissed him.

21) And the son said unto him, Father, I have sinned against heaven, and in thy sight, and am no more worthy to be called thy son.

22) But the father said to his servants, Bring forth the best robe, and put it on him; and put a ring on his hand, and shoes on his feet:

23) And bring hither the fatted calf, and kill it; and let us eat, and be merry:

24) For this my son was dead, and is alive again; he was lost, and is found. And they began to be merry.

25) Now his elder son was in the field: and as he came and drew nigh to the house, he heard music and dancing.

26) And he called one of the servants, and asked what these things meant.

27) And he said unto him, Thy brother is come; and thy father hath killed the fatted calf, because he hath received him safe and sound.

28) And he was angry, and would not go in: therefore came his father out, and entreated him.

29) And he answering said to his father, Lo, these many years do I serve thee, neither transgressed I at any time thy commandment: and yet thou never gavest me a kid, that I might make merry with my friends:

30) But as soon as this thy son was come,

which hath devoured thy living with harlots, thou hast killed for him the fatted calf.

31) And he said unto him, Son, thou art ever with me, and all that I have is thine.

32) It was meet that we should make merry, and be glad: for this thy brother was dead, and is alive again; and was lost, and is found.

Luke 15:1-32

∼ 20 ∼

HOLY SPIRIT

ACTS 2

1) And when the day of Pentecost was fully come, they were all with one accord in one place.

2) And suddenly there came a sound from heaven as of a rushing mighty wind, and it filled all the house where they were sitting.

3) And there appeared unto them cloven tongues like as of fire, and it sat upon each of them.

4) And they were all filled with the Holy Ghost, and began to speak with other tongues, as the Spirit gave them utterance.

5) And there were dwelling at Jerusalem Jews, devout men, out of every nation under heaven.

6) Now when this was noised abroad, the multitude came together, and were confounded, because that every man heard them speak in his own language.

7) And they were all amazed and marvelled, saying one to another, Behold, are not all these which speak Galilaeans?

8) And how hear we every man in our own tongue, wherein we were born?

9) Parthians, and Medes, and Elamites, and

the dwellers in Mesopotamia, and in Judaea, and Cappadocia, in Pontus, and Asia,

10) Phrygia, and Pamphylia, in Egypt, and in the parts of Libya about Cyrene, and strangers of Rome, Jews and proselytes,

11) Cretes and Arabians, we do hear them speak in our tongues the wonderful works of God.

12) And they were all amazed, and were in doubt, saying one to another, What meaneth this?

13) Others mocking said, These men are full of new wine.

14) But Peter, standing up with the eleven, lifted up his voice, and said unto them, Ye men of Judaea, and all ye that dwell at Jerusalem, be this known unto you, and hearken to my words:

15) For these are not drunken, as ye suppose, seeing it is but the third hour of the day.

16) But this is that which was spoken by the prophet Joel;

17) And it shall come to pass in the last days, saith God, I will pour out of My Spirit upon all flesh: and your sons and your daughters shall prophesy, and your young men shall see visions, and your old men shall dream dreams:

18) And on My servants and on My handmaidens I will pour out in those days of My Spirit; and they shall prophesy:

19) And I will shew wonders in heaven above, and signs in the earth beneath; blood, and fire, and vapour of smoke:

20) The sun shall be turned into darkness, and the moon into blood, before that great and notable day of the Lord come:

21) And it shall come to pass, that whosoever shall call on the name of the Lord shall be saved.

22) Ye men of Israel, hear these words; Jesus of Nazareth, a man approved of God among you by miracles and wonders and signs, which God did by Him in the midst of you, as ye yourselves also know:

23) Him, being delivered by the determinate counsel and foreknowledge of God, ye have taken, and by wicked hands have crucified and slain:

24) Whom God hath raised up, having loosed the pains of death: because it was not possible that He should be holden of it.

25) For David speaketh concerning Him, I foresaw the Lord always before my face, for He is on my right hand, that I should not be moved:

26) Therefore did my heart rejoice, and my tongue was glad; moreover also my flesh shall rest in hope:

27) Because Thou wilt not leave my soul in hell, neither wilt Thou suffer Thine Holy One to see corruption.

28) Thou hast made known to me the ways of life; Thou shalt make me full of joy with Thy countenance.

29) Men and brethren, let me freely speak unto you of the patriarch David, that He is both dead and buried, and His sepulchre is with us unto this day.

30) Therefore being a prophet, and knowing that God had sworn with an oath to Him, that of the fruit of His loins, according to the flesh, He would raise up Christ to sit on His throne;

31) He seeing this before spake of the resurrection of Christ, that His soul was not left in hell, neither His flesh did see corruption.

32) This Jesus hath God raised up, whereof we all are witnesses.

33) Therefore being by the right hand of God exalted, and having received of the Father the promise of the Holy Ghost, He hath shed forth this, which ye now see and hear.

34) For David is not ascended into the heavens: but he saith himself, The Lord said unto my Lord, Sit Thou on My right hand,

35) Until I make Thy foes Thy footstool.

36) Therefore let all the house of Israel know assuredly, that God hath made that same Jesus, Whom ye have crucified, both Lord and Christ.

37) Now when they heard this, they were pricked in their heart, and said unto Peter and to the rest of the apostles, Men and brethren, what shall we do?

38) Then Peter said unto them, Repent, and be baptized every one of you in the name of Jesus Christ for the remission of sins, and ye shall receive the gift of the Holy Ghost.

39) For the promise is unto you, and to your children, and to all that are afar off, even as many as the Lord our God shall call.

40) And with many other words did he testify and exhort, saying, Save yourselves from this untoward generation.

41) Then they that gladly received his word were baptized: and the same day there were added unto them about three thousand souls.

42) And they continued stedfastly in the apostles' doctrine and fellowship, and in breaking of bread, and in prayers.

43) And fear came upon every soul: and many wonders and signs were done by the apostles.

44) And all that believed were together, and had all things common;

45) And sold their possessions and goods, and parted them to all men, as every man had need.

46) And they, continuing daily with one accord in the temple, and breaking bread from house to house, did eat their meat with gladness and singleness of heart,

47) Praising God, and having favour with all the people. And the Lord added to the church daily such as should be saved.   *Acts 2:1-47*

God Never Consults
Your Past
To Determine
Your Future.

-MIKE MURDOCK

~ 21 ~

JUSTIFIED BY FAITH

ROMANS 1

1) Paul, a servant of Jesus Christ, called to be an apostle, separated unto the gospel of God,

2) Which He had promised afore by His prophets in the holy scriptures,

3) Concerning His Son Jesus Christ our Lord, which was made of the seed of David according to the flesh;

4) And declared to be the Son of God with power, according to the spirit of holiness, by the resurrection from the dead:

5) By Whom we have received grace and apostleship, for obedience to the faith among all nations, for His name:

6) Among Whom are ye also the called of Jesus Christ:

7) To all that be in Rome, beloved of God, called to be saints: Grace to you and peace from God our Father, and the Lord Jesus Christ.

8) First, I thank my God through Jesus Christ for you all, that your faith is spoken of throughout the whole world.

9) For God is my witness, Whom I serve with my spirit in the gospel of His Son, that without

ceasing I make mention of you always in my prayers;

10) Making request, if by any means now at length I might have a prosperous journey by the will of God to come unto you.

11) For I long to see you, that I may impart unto you some spiritual gift, to the end ye may be established;

12) That is, that I may be comforted together with you by the mutual faith both of you and me.

13) Now I would not have you ignorant, brethren, that oftentimes I purposed to come unto you, but was let hitherto, that I might have some fruit among you also, even as among other Gentiles.

14) I am debtor both to the Greeks, and to the Barbarians; both to the wise, and to the unwise.

15) So, as much as in me is, I am ready to preach the gospel to you that are at Rome also.

16) For I am not ashamed of the gospel of Christ: for it is the power of God unto salvation to every one that believeth; to the Jew first, and also to the Greek.

17) For therein is the righteousness of God revealed from faith to faith: as it is written, The just shall live by faith.

18) For the wrath of God is revealed from heaven against all ungodliness and unrighteousness of men, who hold the truth in unrighteousness;

19) Because that which may be known of God is manifest in them; for God hath shewed it unto them.

20) For the invisible things of Him from the creation of the world are clearly seen, being understood by the things that are made, even His eternal power and Godhead; so that they are without excuse:

21) Because that, when they knew God, they glorified Him not as God, neither were thankful; but became vain in their imaginations, and their foolish heart was darkened.

22) Professing themselves to be wise, they became fools,

23) And changed the glory of the uncorruptible God into an image made like to corruptible man, and to birds, and fourfooted beasts, and creeping things.

24) Wherefore God also gave them up to uncleanness through the lusts of their own hearts, to dishonour their own bodies between themselves:

25) Who changed the truth of God into a lie, and worshipped and served the creature more than the Creator, Who is blessed for ever. Amen.

26) For this cause God gave them up unto vile affections: for even their women did change the natural use into that which is against nature:

27) And likewise also the men, leaving the natural use of the woman, burned in their lust one toward another; men with men working that which is unseemly, and receiving in themselves that recompence of their error which was meet.

28) And even as they did not like to retain God in their knowledge, God gave them over to a reprobate mind, to do those things which are not convenient;

29) Being filled with all unrighteousness,

fornication, wickedness, covetousness, maliciousness; full of envy, murder, debate, deceit, malignity; whisperers,

30) Backbiters, haters of God, despiteful, proud, boasters, inventors of evil things, disobedient to parents,

31) Without understanding, covenantbreakers, without natural affection, implacable, unmerciful:

32) Who knowing the judgment of God, that they which commit such things are worthy of death, not only do the same, but have pleasure in them that do them.   *Romans 1:1-32*

≈ 22 ≈

LOVE OF GOD

ROMANS 8

1) There is therefore now no condemnation to them which are in Christ Jesus, who walk not after the flesh, but after the Spirit.

2) For the law of the Spirit of life in Christ Jesus hath made me free from the law of sin and death.

3) For what the law could not do, in that it was weak through the flesh, God sending His own Son in the likeness of sinful flesh, and for sin, condemned sin in the flesh:

4) That the righteousness of the law might be fulfilled in us, who walk not after the flesh, but after the Spirit.

5) For they that are after the flesh do mind the things of the flesh; but they that are after the Spirit the things of the Spirit.

6) For to be carnally minded is death; but to be spiritually minded is life and peace.

7) Because the carnal mind is enmity against God: for it is not subject to the law of God, neither indeed can be.

8) So then they that are in the flesh cannot please God.

9) But ye are not in the flesh, but in the Spirit, if so be that the Spirit of God dwell in you. Now if any man have not the Spirit of Christ, he is none of His.

10) And if Christ be in you, the body is dead because of sin; but the Spirit is life because of righteousness.

11) But if the Spirit of Him that raised up Jesus from the dead dwell in you, He that raised up Christ from the dead shall also quicken your mortal bodies by His Spirit that dwelleth in you.

12) Therefore, brethren, we are debtors, not to the flesh, to live after the flesh.

13) For if ye live after the flesh, ye shall die: but if ye through the Spirit do mortify the deeds of the body, ye shall live.

14) For as many as are led by the Spirit of God, they are the sons of God.

15) For ye have not received the spirit of bondage again to fear; but ye have received the Spirit of adoption, whereby we cry, Abba, Father.

16) The Spirit itself beareth witness with our spirit, that we are the children of God:

17) And if children, then heirs; heirs of God, and joint-heirs with Christ; if so be that we suffer with Him, that we may be also glorified together.

18) For I reckon that the sufferings of this present time are not worthy to be compared with the glory which shall be revealed in us.

19) For the earnest expectation of the creature waiteth for the manifestation of the sons of God.

20) For the creature was made subject to

vanity, not willingly, but by reason of Him who hath subjected the same in hope,

21) Because the creature itself also shall be delivered from the bondage of corruption into the glorious liberty of the children of God.

22) For we know that the whole creation groaneth and travaileth in pain together until now.

23) And not only they, but ourselves also, which have the firstfruits of the Spirit, even we ourselves groan within ourselves, waiting for the adoption, to wit, the redemption of our body.

24) For we are saved by hope: but hope that is seen is not hope: for what a man seeth, why doth he yet hope for?

25) But if we hope for that we see not, then do we with patience wait for it.

26) Likewise the Spirit also helpeth our infirmities: for we know not what we should pray for as we ought: but the Spirit itself maketh intercession for us with groanings which cannot be uttered.

27) And He that searcheth the hearts knoweth what is the mind of the Spirit, because He maketh intercession for the saints according to the will of God.

28) And we know that all things work together for good to them that love God, to them who are the called according to His purpose.

29) For whom He did foreknow, He also did predestinate to be conformed to the image of His Son, that He might be the firstborn among many brethren.

30) Moreover whom He did predestinate,

them He also called: and whom He called, them He also justified: and whom He justified, them He also glorified.

31) What shall we then say to these things? If God be for us, who can be against us?

32) He that spared not His own Son, but delivered Him up for us all, how shall He not with Him also freely give us all things?

33) Who shall lay any thing to the charge of God's elect? It is God that justifieth.

34) Who is he that condemneth? It is Christ that died, yea rather, that is risen again, Who is even at the right hand of God, Who also maketh intercession for us.

35) Who shall separate us from the love of Christ? shall tribulation, or distress, or persecution, or famine, or nakedness, or peril, or sword?

36) As it is written, For Thy sake we are killed all the day long; we are accounted as sheep for the slaughter.

37) Nay, in all these things we are more than conquerors through Him that loved us.

38) For I am persuaded, that neither death, nor life, nor angels, nor principalities, nor powers, nor things present, nor things to come,

39) Nor height, nor depth, nor any other creature, shall be able to separate us from the love of God, which is in Christ Jesus our Lord.

Romans 8:1-39

❧ 23 ❧

MARRIAGE

1 CORINTHIANS 7

1) Now concerning the things whereof ye wrote unto me: It is good for a man not to touch a woman.

2) Nevertheless, to avoid fornication, let every man have his own wife, and let every woman have her own husband.

3) Let the husband render unto the wife due benevolence: and likewise also the wife unto the husband.

4) The wife hath not power of her own body, but the husband: and likewise also the husband hath not power of his own body, but the wife.

5) Defraud ye not one the other, except it be with consent for a time, that ye may give yourselves to fasting and prayer; and come together again, that satan tempt you not for your incontinency.

6) But I speak this by permission, and not of commandment.

7) For I would that all men were even as I myself. But every man hath his proper gift of God, one after this manner, and another after that.

8) I say therefore to the unmarried and

widows, It is good for them if they abide even as I.

9) But if they cannot contain, let them marry: for it is better to marry than to burn.

10) And unto the married I command, yet not I, but the Lord, Let not the wife depart from her husband:

11) But and if she depart, let her remain unmarried, or be reconciled to her husband: and let not the husband put away his wife.

12) But to the rest speak I, not the Lord: If any brother hath a wife that believeth not, and she be pleased to dwell with him, let him not put her away.

13) And the woman which hath an husband that believeth not, and if he be pleased to dwell with her, let her not leave him.

14) For the unbelieving husband is sanctified by the wife, and the unbelieving wife is sanctified by the husband: else were your children unclean; but now are they holy.

15) But if the unbelieving depart, let him depart. A brother or a sister is not under bondage in such cases: but God hath called us to peace.

16) For what knowest thou, O wife, whether thou shalt save thy husband? or how knowest thou, O man, whether thou shalt save thy wife?

17) But as God hath distributed to every man, as the Lord hath called every one, so let him walk. And so ordain I in all churches.

18) Is any man called being circumcised? let him not become uncircumcised. Is any called in uncircumcision? let him not be circumcised.

19) Circumcision is nothing, and uncircumcision is nothing, but the keeping of the commandments of God.

20) Let every man abide in the same calling wherein he was called.

21) Art thou called being a servant? care not for it: but if thou mayest be made free, use it rather.

22) For he that is called in the Lord, being a servant, is the Lord's freeman: likewise also he that is called, being free, is Christ's servant.

23) Ye are bought with a price; be not ye the servants of men.

24) Brethren, let every man, wherein he is called, therein abide with God.

25) Now concerning virgins I have no commandment of the Lord: yet I give my judgment, as one that hath obtained mercy of the Lord to be faithful.

26) I suppose therefore that this is good for the present distress, I say, that it is good for a man so to be.

27) Art thou bound unto a wife? seek not to be loosed. Art thou loosed from a wife? seek not a wife.

28) But and if thou marry, thou hast not sinned; and if a virgin marry, she hath not sinned. Nevertheless such shall have trouble in the flesh: but I spare you.

29) But this I say, brethren, the time is short: it remaineth, that both they that have wives be as though they had none;

30) And they that weep, as though they wept not; and they that rejoice, as though they rejoiced not; and they that buy, as though they possessed not;

31) And they that use this world, as not abusing it: for the fashion of this world passeth

away.

32) But I would have you without carefulness. He that is unmarried careth for the things that belong to the Lord, how he may please the Lord:

33) But he that is married careth for the things that are of the world, how he may please his wife.

34) There is difference also between a wife and a virgin. The unmarried woman careth for the things of the Lord, that she may be holy both in body and in spirit: but she that is married careth for the things of the world, how she may please her husband.

35) And this I speak for your own profit; not that I may cast a snare upon you, but for that which is comely, and that ye may attend upon the Lord without distraction.

36) But if any man think that he behaveth himself uncomely toward his virgin, if she pass the flower of her age, and need so require, let him do what he will, he sinneth not: let them marry.

37) Nevertheless he that standeth stedfast in his heart, having no necessity, but hath power over his own will, and hath so decreed in his heart that he will keep his virgin, doeth well.

38) So then he that giveth her in marriage doeth well; but he that giveth her not in marriage doeth better.

39) The wife is bound by the law as long as her husband liveth; but if her husband be dead, she is at liberty to be married to whom she will; only in the Lord.

40) But she is happier if she so abide, after my judgment: and I think also that I have the Spirit of God.   *1 Corinthians 7:1-40*

❧ 24 ❧

LOVE

1 CORINTHIANS 13

1) Though I speak with the tongues of men and of angels, and have not charity, I am become as sounding brass, or a tinkling cymbal.

2) And though I have the gift of prophecy, and understand all mysteries, and all knowledge; and though I have all faith, so that I could remove mountains, and have not charity, I am nothing.

3) And though I bestow all my goods to feed the poor, and though I give my body to be burned, and have not charity, it profiteth me nothing.

4) Charity suffereth long, and is kind; charity envieth not; charity vaunteth not itself, is not puffed up,

5) Doth not behave itself unseemly, seeketh not her own, is not easily provoked, thinketh no evil;

6) Rejoiceth not in iniquity, but rejoiceth in the truth;

7) Beareth all things, believeth all things, hopeth all things, endureth all things.

8) Charity never faileth: but whether there be prophecies, they shall fail; whether there be tongues, they shall cease; whether there be

knowledge, it shall vanish away.

9) For we know in part, and we prophesy in part.

10) But when that which is perfect is come, then that which is in part shall be done away.

11) When I was a child, I spake as a child, I understood as a child, I thought as a child: but when I became a man, I put away childish things.

12) For now we see through a glass, darkly; but then face to face: now I know in part; but then shall I know even as also I am known.

13) And now abideth faith, hope, charity, these three; but the greatest of these is charity.

1 Corinthians 13:1-13

∻ 25 ∻

THE PRAYER LANGUAGE

1 CORINTHIANS 14

1) Follow after charity, and desire spiritual gifts, but rather that ye may prophesy.

2) For he that speaketh in an unknown tongue speaketh not unto men, but unto God: for no man understandeth him; howbeit in the spirit he speaketh mysteries.

3) But he that prophesieth speaketh unto men to edification, and exhortation, and comfort.

4) He that speaketh in an unknown tongue edifieth himself; but he that prophesieth edifieth the church.

5) I would that ye all spake with tongues; but rather that ye prophesied: for greater is he that prophesieth than he that speaketh with tongues, except he interpret, that the church may receive edifying.

6) Now, brethren, if I come unto you speaking with tongues, what shall I profit you, except I shall speak to you either by revelation, or by knowledge, or by prophesying, or by doctrine?

7) And even things without life giving sound, whether pipe or harp, except they give a distinction in the sounds, how shall it be known what is piped

or harped?

8) For if the trumpet give an uncertain sound, who shall prepare himself to the battle?

9) So likewise ye, except ye utter by the tongue words easy to be understood, how shall it be known what is spoken? for ye shall speak into the air.

10) There are, it may be, so many kinds of voices in the world, and none of them is without signification.

11) Therefore if I know not the meaning of the voice, I shall be unto him that speaketh a barbarian, and he that speaketh shall be a barbarian unto me.

12) Even so ye, forasmuch as ye are zealous of spiritual gifts, seek that ye may excel to the edifying of the church.

13) Wherefore let him that speaketh in an unknown tongue pray that he may interpret.

14) For if I pray in an unknown tongue, my spirit prayeth, but my understanding is unfruitful.

15) What is it then? I will pray with the spirit, and I will pray with the understanding also: I will sing with the spirit, and I will sing with the understanding also.

16) Else when thou shalt bless with the spirit, how shall he that occupieth the room of the unlearned say Amen at thy giving of thanks, seeing he understandeth not what thou sayest?

17) For thou verily givest thanks well, but the other is not edified.

18) I thank my God, I speak with tongues more than ye all:

19) Yet in the church I had rather speak five words with my understanding, that by my voice I might teach others also, than ten thousand words in an unknown tongue.

20) Brethren, be not children in understanding: howbeit in malice be ye children, but in understanding be men.

21) In the law it is written, With men of other tongues and other lips will I speak unto this people; and yet for all that will they not hear me, saith the Lord.

22) Wherefore tongues are for a sign, not to them that believe, but to them that believe not: but prophesying serveth not for them that believe not, but for them which believe.

23) If therefore the whole church be come together into one place, and all speak with tongues, and there come in those that are unlearned, or unbelievers, will they not say that ye are mad?

24) But if all prophesy, and there come in one that believeth not, or one unlearned, he is convinced of all, he is judged of all:

25) And thus are the secrets of his heart made manifest; and so falling down on his face, he will worship God, and report that God is in you of a truth.

26) How is it then, brethren? when ye come together, every one of you hath a psalm, hath a doctrine, hath a tongue, hath a revelation, hath an interpretation. Let all things be done unto edifying.

27) If any man speak in an unknown tongue, let it be by two, or at the most by three, and that by

course; and let one interpret.

28) But if there be no interpreter, let him keep silence in the church; and let him speak to himself, and to God.

29) Let the prophets speak two or three, and let the other judge.

30) If any thing be revealed to another that sitteth by, let the first hold his peace.

31) For ye may all prophesy one by one, that all may learn, and all may be comforted.

32) And the spirits of the prophets are subject to the prophets.

33) For God is not the author of confusion, but of peace, as in all churches of the saints.

34) Let your women keep silence in the churches: for it is not permitted unto them to speak; but they are commanded to be under obedience, as also saith the law.

35) And if they will learn any thing, let them ask their husbands at home: for it is a shame for women to speak in the church.

36) What? came the word of God out from you? or came it unto you only?

37) If any man think himself to be a prophet, or spiritual, let him acknowledge that the things that I write unto you are the commandments of the Lord.

38) But if any man be ignorant, let him be ignorant.

39) Wherefore, brethren, covet to prophesy, and forbid not to speak with tongues.

40) Let all things be done decently and in order.   *1 Corinthians 14:1-40*

❧ 26 ❧

FRUIT OF THE SPIRIT

GALATIANS 5

1) Stand fast therefore in the liberty wherewith Christ hath made us free, and be not entangled again with the yoke of bondage.

2) Behold, I Paul say unto you, that if ye be circumcised, Christ shall profit you nothing.

3) For I testify again to every man that is circumcised, that he is a debtor to do the whole law.

4) Christ is become of no effect unto you, whosoever of you are justified by the law; ye are fallen from grace.

5) For we through the Spirit wait for the hope of righteousness by faith.

6) For in Jesus Christ neither circumcision availeth any thing, nor uncircumcision; but faith which worketh by love.

7) Ye did run well; who did hinder you that ye should not obey the truth?

8) This persuasion cometh not of Him that calleth you.

9) A little leaven leaveneth the whole lump.

10) I have confidence in you through the Lord, that ye will be none otherwise minded: but he that troubleth you shall bear his judgment, whosoever

he be.

11) And I, brethren, if I yet preach circumcision, why do I yet suffer persecution? then is the offence of the cross ceased.

12) I would they were even cut off which trouble you.

13) For, brethren, ye have been called unto liberty; only use not liberty for an occasion to the flesh, but by love serve one another.

14) For all the law is fulfilled in one word, even in this; Thou shalt love thy neighbour as thyself.

15) But if ye bite and devour one another, take heed that ye be not consumed one of another.

16) This I say then, Walk in the Spirit, and ye shall not fulfil the lust of the flesh.

17) For the flesh lusteth against the Spirit, and the Spirit against the flesh: and these are contrary the one to the other: so that ye cannot do the things that ye would.

18) But if ye be led of the Spirit, ye are not under the law.

19) Now the works of the flesh are manifest, which are these; Adultery, fornication, uncleanness, lasciviousness,

20) Idolatry, witchcraft, hatred, variance, emulations, wrath, strife, seditions, heresies,

21) Envyings, murders, drunkenness, revellings, and such like: of the which I tell you before, as I have also told you in time past, that they which do such things shall not inherit the kingdom of God.

22) But the fruit of the Spirit is love, joy,

peace, longsuffering, gentleness, goodness, faith,

23) Meekness, temperance: against such there is no law.

24) And they that are Christ's have crucified the flesh with the affections and lusts.

25) If we live in the Spirit, let us also walk in the Spirit.

26) Let us not be desirous of vain glory, provoking one another, envying one another.

Galatians 5:1-26

Your Rewards In Life
Are Determined
By The Kinds Of Problems
You Are Willing
To Solve For Others.

-MIKE MURDOCK

❧ 27 ❧

GREATEST LAW OF EARTH

GALATIANS 6

1) Brethren, if a man be overtaken in a fault, ye which are spiritual, restore such an one in the spirit of meekness; considering thyself, lest thou also be tempted.

2) Bear ye one another's burdens, and so fulfil the law of Christ.

3) For if a man think himself to be something, when he is nothing, he deceiveth himself.

4) But let every man prove his own work, and then shall he have rejoicing in himself alone, and not in another.

5) For every man shall bear his own burden.

6) Let him that is taught in the word communicate unto him that teacheth in all good things.

7) Be not deceived; God is not mocked: for whatsoever a man soweth, that shall he also reap.

8) For he that soweth to his flesh shall of the flesh reap corruption; but he that soweth to the Spirit shall of the Spirit reap life everlasting.

9) And let us not be weary in well doing: for in due season we shall reap, if we faint not.

10) As we have therefore opportunity, let us do good unto all men, especially unto them who are of the household of faith.

11) Ye see how large a letter I have written unto you with mine own hand.

12) As many as desire to make a fair shew in the flesh, they constrain you to be circumcised; only lest they should suffer persecution for the cross of Christ.

13) For neither they themselves who are circumcised keep the law; but desire to have you circumcised, that they may glory in your flesh.

14) But God forbid that I should glory, save in the cross of our Lord Jesus Christ, by Whom the world is crucified unto me, and I unto the world.

15) For in Christ Jesus neither circumcision availeth any thing, nor uncircumcision, but a new creature.

16) And as many as walk according to this rule, peace be on them, and mercy, and upon the Israel of God.

17) From henceforth let no man trouble me: for I bear in my body the marks of the Lord Jesus.

18) Brethren, the grace of our Lord Jesus Christ be with your spirit. Amen.

Galatians 6:1-18

28

FAITH

HEBREWS 11

1)   Now faith is the substance of things hoped for, the evidence of things not seen.

2)   For by it the elders obtained a good report.

3)   Through faith we understand that the worlds were framed by the word of God, so that things which are seen were not made of things which do appear.

4)   By faith Abel offered unto God a more excellent sacrifice than Cain, by which he obtained witness that he was righteous, God testifying of his gifts: and by it He being dead yet speaketh.

5)   By faith Enoch was translated that he should not see death; and was not found, because God had translated him: for before his translation he had this testimony, that he pleased God.

6)   But without faith it is impossible to please Him: for he that cometh to God must believe that He is, and that He is a rewarder of them that diligently seek Him.

7)   By faith Noah, being warned of God of things not seen as yet, moved with fear, prepared an ark to the saving of his house; by the which he condemned the world, and became heir of the

righteousness which is by faith.

8) By faith Abraham, when he was called to go out into a place which he should after receive for an inheritance, obeyed; and he went out, not knowing whither he went.

9) By faith he sojourned in the land of promise, as in a strange country, dwelling in tabernacles with Isaac and Jacob, the heirs with him of the same promise:

10) For he looked for a city which hath foundations, whose builder and maker is God.

11) Through faith also Sara herself received strength to conceive seed, and was delivered of a child when she was past age, because she judged Him faithful who had promised.

12) Therefore sprang there even of one, and Him as good as dead, so many as the stars of the sky in multitude, and as the sand which is by the sea shore innumerable.

13) These all died in faith, not having received the promises, but having seen them afar off, and were persuaded of them, and embraced them, and confessed that they were strangers and pilgrims on the earth.

14) For they that say such things declare plainly that they seek a country.

15) And truly, if they had been mindful of that country from whence they came out, they might have had opportunity to have returned.

16) But now they desire a better country, that is, an heavenly: wherefore God is not ashamed to be called their God: for He hath prepared for them a city.

17) By faith Abraham, when he was tried, offered up Isaac; and He that had received the promises offered up His only begotten Son,

18) Of Whom it was said, That in Isaac shall Thy seed be called:

19) Accounting that God was able to raise Him up, even from the dead; from whence also He received Him in a figure.

20) By faith Isaac blessed Jacob and Esau concerning things to come.

21) By faith Jacob, when he was a dying, blessed both the sons of Joseph; and worshipped, leaning upon the top of his staff.

22) By faith Joseph, when he died, made mention of the departing of the children of Israel; and gave commandment concerning his bones.

23) By faith Moses, when he was born, was hid three months of his parents, because they saw he was a proper child; and they were not afraid of the king's commandment.

24) By faith Moses, when he was come to years, refused to be called the son of Pharaoh's daughter;

25) Choosing rather to suffer affliction with the people of God, than to enjoy the pleasures of sin for a season;

26) Esteeming the reproach of Christ greater riches than the treasures in Egypt: for he had respect unto the recompence of the reward.

27) By faith he forsook Egypt, not fearing the wrath of the king: for he endured, as seeing him who is invisible.

28) Through faith he kept the passover, and

the sprinkling of blood, lest he that destroyed the firstborn should touch them.

29) By faith they passed through the Red sea as by dry land: which the Egyptians assaying to do were drowned.

30) By faith the walls of Jericho fell down, after they were compassed about seven days.

31) By faith the harlot Rahab perished not with them that believed not, when she had received the spies with peace.

32) And what shall I more say? for the time would fail me to tell of Gedeon, and of Barak, and of Samson, and of Jephthae; of David also, and Samuel, and of the prophets:

33) Who through faith subdued kingdoms, wrought righteousness, obtained promises, stopped the mouths of lions.

34) Quenched the violence of fire, escaped the edge of the sword, out of weakness were made strong, waxed valiant in fight, turned to flight the armies of the aliens.

35) Women received their dead raised to life again: and others were tortured, not accepting deliverance; that they might obtain a better resurrection:

36) And others had trial of cruel mockings and scourgings, yea, moreover of bonds and imprisonment:

37) They were stoned, they were sawn asunder, were tempted, were slain with the sword: they wandered about in sheepskins and goatskins; being destitute, afflicted, tormented;

38) Of whom the world was not worthy: they

wandered in deserts, and in mountains, and in dens and caves of the earth.

39) And these all, having obtained a good report through faith, received not the promise:

40) God having provided some better thing for us, that they without us should not be made perfect. *Hebrews 11:1-40*

You Will Never
Reach The Palace,
Talking Like A Peasant.

-MIKE MURDOCK

∾ 29 ∾

THE TONGUE —
SECRET OF PERFECTION

━━━━━━>•◦•<━━━━━━

JAMES 3

1) My brethren, be not many masters, knowing that we shall receive the greater condemnation.

2) For in many things we offend all. If any man offend not in word, the same is a perfect man, and able also to bridle the whole body.

3) Behold, we put bits in the horses' mouths, that they may obey us; and we turn about their whole body.

4) Behold also the ships, which though they be so great, and are driven of fierce winds, yet are they turned about with a very small helm, whithersoever the governor listeth.

5) Even so the tongue is a little member, and boasteth great things. Behold, how great a matter a little fire kindleth!

6) And the tongue is a fire, a world of iniquity: so is the tongue among our members, that it defileth the whole body, and setteth on fire the course of nature; and it is set on fire of hell.

7) For every kind of beasts, and of birds, and

of serpents, and of things in the sea, is tamed, and hath been tamed of mankind:

8) But the tongue can no man tame; it is an unruly evil, full of deadly poison.

9) Therewith bless we God, even the Father; and therewith curse we men, which are made after the similitude of God.

10) Out of the same mouth proceedeth blessing and cursing. My brethren, these things ought not so to be.

11) Doth a fountain send forth at the same place sweet water and bitter?

12) Can the fig tree, my brethren, bear olive berries? either a vine, figs? so can no fountain both yield salt water and fresh.

13) Who is a wise man and endued with knowledge among you? let him shew out of a good conversation his works with meekness of wisdom.

14) But if ye have bitter envying and strife in your hearts, glory not, and lie not against the truth.

15) This wisdom descendeth not from above, but is earthly, sensual, devilish.

16) For where envying and strife is, there is confusion and every evil work.

17) But the wisdom that is from above is first pure, then peaceable, gentle, and easy to be entreated, full of mercy and good fruits, without partiality, and without hypocrisy.

18) And the fruit of righteousness is sown in peace of them that make peace.   *James 3:1-18*

~ 30 ~

Satan's Defeat

REVELATION 20

1) And I saw an angel come down from heaven, having the key of the bottomless pit and a great chain in his hand.

2) And he laid hold on the dragon, that old serpent, which is the devil, and satan, and bound him a thousand years,

3) And cast him into the bottomless pit, and shut him up, and set a seal upon him, that he should deceive the nations no more, till the thousand years should be fulfilled: and after that he must be loosed a little season.

4) And I saw thrones, and they sat upon them, and judgment was given unto them: and I saw the souls of them that were beheaded for the witness of Jesus, and for the word of God, and which had not worshipped the beast, neither his image, neither had received his mark upon their foreheads, or in their hands; and they lived and reigned with Christ a thousand years.

5) But the rest of the dead lived not again until the thousand years were finished. This is the first resurrection.

6) Blessed and holy is he that hath part in the first resurrection: on such the second death

hath no power, but they shall be priests of God and of Christ, and shall reign with Him a thousand years.

7) And when the thousand years are expired, satan shall be loosed out of his prison,

8) And shall go out to deceive the nations which are in the four quarters of the earth, Gog, and Magog, to gather them together to battle: the number of whom is as the sand of the sea.

9) And they went up on the breadth of the earth, and compassed the camp of the saints about, and the beloved city: and fire came down from God out of heaven, and devoured them.

10) And the devil that deceived them was cast into the lake of fire and brimstone, where the beast and the false prophet are, and shall be tormented day and night for ever and ever.

11) And I saw a great white throne, and him that sat on it, from whose face the earth and the heaven fled away; and there was found no place for them.

12) And I saw the dead, small and great, stand before God; and the books were opened: and another book was opened, which is the book of life: and the dead were judged out of those things which were written in the books, according to their works.

13) And the sea gave up the dead which were in it; and death and hell delivered up the dead which were in them: and they were judged every man according to their works.

14) And death and hell were cast into the lake of fire. This is the second death.

15) And whosoever was not found written in the book of life was cast into the lake of fire.

Revelation 20:1-15

～ 31 ～
NEW HEAVEN AND NEW EARTH

REVELATION 21

1) And I saw a new heaven and a new earth: for the first heaven and the first earth were passed away; and there was no more sea.

2) And I John saw the holy city, new Jerusalem, coming down from God out of heaven, prepared as a bride adorned for her husband.

3) And I heard a great voice out of heaven saying, Behold, the tabernacle of God is with men, and He will dwell with them, and they shall be His people, and God Himself shall be with them, and be their God.

4) And God shall wipe away all tears from their eyes; and there shall be no more death, neither sorrow, nor crying, neither shall there be any more pain: for the former things are passed away.

5) And he that sat upon the throne said, Behold, I make all things new. And He said unto me, Write: for these words are true and faithful.

6) And He said unto me, It is done. I am Alpha and Omega, the beginning and the end. I

will give unto him that is athirst of the fountain of the water of life freely.

7) He that overcometh shall inherit all things; and I will be his God, and he shall be My son.

8) But the fearful, and unbelieving, and abominable, and murderers, and whoremongers, and sorcerers, and idolaters, and all liars, shall have their part in the lake which burneth with fire and brimstone: which is the second death.

9) And there came unto me one of the seven angels which had the seven vials full of the seven last plagues, and talked with me, saying, Come hither, I will shew thee the bride, the Lamb's wife.

10) And he carried me away in the spirit to a great and high mountain, and shewed me that great city, the holy Jerusalem, descending out of heaven from God,

11) Having the glory of God: and her light was like unto a stone most precious, even like a jasper stone, clear as crystal;

12) And had a wall great and high, and had twelve gates, and at the gates twelve angels, and names written thereon, which are the names of the twelve tribes of the children of Israel:

13) On the east three gates; on the north three gates; on the south three gates; and on the west three gates.

14) And the wall of the city had twelve foundations, and in them the names of the twelve apostles of the Lamb.

15) And he that talked with me had a golden reed to measure the city, and the gates thereof, and the wall thereof.

16) And the city lieth foursquare, and the length is as large as the breadth: and he measured the city with the reed, twelve thousand furlongs. The length and the breadth and the height of it are equal.

17) And he measured the wall thereof, an hundred and forty and four cubits, according to the measure of a man, that is, of the angel.

18) And the building of the wall of it was of jasper: and the city was pure gold, like unto clear glass.

19) And the foundations of the wall of the city were garnished with all manner of precious stones. The first foundation was jasper; the second, sapphire; the third, a chalcedony; the fourth, an emerald,

20) The fifth, sardonyx; the sixth, sardius; the seventh, chrysolyte; the eighth, beryl; the ninth, a topaz; the tenth, a chrysoprasus; the eleventh, a jacinth; the twelfth, an amethyst.

21) And the twelve gates were twelve pearls: every several gate was of one pearl: and the street of the city was pure gold, as it were transparent glass.

22) And I saw no temple therein: for the Lord God Almighty and the Lamb are the temple of it.

23) And the city had no need of the sun, neither of the moon, to shine in it: for the glory of God did lighten it, and the Lamb is the light thereof.

24) And the nations of them which are saved shall walk in the light of it: and the kings of the earth do bring their glory and honour into it.

25) And the gates of it shall not be shut at all

by day: for there shall be no night there.

26) And they shall bring the glory and honour of the nations into it.

27) And there shall in no wise enter into it any thing that defileth, neither whatsoever worketh abomination, or maketh a lie: but they which are written in the Lamb's book of life.

Revelation 21:1-27

DECISION

Will You Accept Jesus As Your Personal Savior Today?

The Bible says, "That if thou shalt confess with thy mouth the Lord Jesus, and shalt believe in thine heart that God hath raised Him from the dead, thou shalt be saved" (Rom. 10:9).

Pray this prayer from your heart today!

"Dear Jesus, I believe that you died for me and rose again on the third day. I confess I am a sinner...I need Your love and forgiveness...Come into my heart. Forgive my sins. I receive Your eternal life. Confirm Your love by giving me peace, joy and supernatural love for others. Amen."

Clip and Mail

DR. MIKE MURDOCK

is in tremendous demand as one of the most dynamic speakers in America today.

More than 14,000 audiences in 38 countries have attended his Schools of Wisdom. Hundreds of invitations come to him from churches, colleges, and business corporations. He is a noted author of over 130 books, including the best sellers, *"The Leadership Secrets of Jesus"* and *"Secrets of the Richest Man Who Ever Lived."* Thousands view his weekly television program, *"Wisdom Keys with Mike Murdock."* Many attend his Saturday School of Wisdom Breakfasts that he hosts in major cities of America.

☐ Yes, Mike! I made a decision to accept Christ as my personal Savior today. Please send me my free gift of your book, *"31 Keys to a New Beginning"* to help me with my new life in Christ. *(B48)*

NAME _____ BIRTHDAY _____

ADDRESS _____

CITY _____ STATE ____ ZIP _____

PHONE _____ E-MAIL _____ *B-54*

Mail form to:
The Wisdom Center · P. O. Box 99 · Denton, TX 76202
1-888-WISDOM-1 (1-888-947-3661) · Website: www.thewisdomcenter.cc

DR. MIKE MURDOCK

1 Has embraced his Assignment to Pursue...Proclaim...and Publish the Wisdom of God to help people achieve their dreams and goals.

2 Began full-time evangelism at the age of 19, which has continued since 1966.

3 Has traveled and spoken to more than 14,000 audiences in 38 countries, including East and West Africa, the Orient and Europe.

4 Noted author of 130 books, including best sellers, "Wisdom For Winning," "Dream Seeds" and "The Double Diamond Principle."

5 Created the popular "Topical Bible" series for Businessmen, Mothers, Fathers, Teenagers; "The One-Minute Pocket Bible" series, and "The Uncommon Life" series.

6 Has composed more than 5,700 songs such as "I Am Blessed," "You Can Make It," "God Rides On Wings Of Love" and "Jesus, Just The Mention Of Your Name," recorded by many gospel artists.

7 Is the Founder of The Wisdom Center, in Denton, Texas.

8 Has a weekly television program called "Wisdom Keys With Mike Murdock."

9 Has appeared often on TBN, CBN and other television network programs.

10 Is a Founding Trustee on the Board of International Charismatic Bible Ministries with Oral Roberts.

11 Has had more than 3,500 accept the call into full-time ministry under his ministry.

THE MINISTRY

1 **Wisdom Books & Literature** - Over 130 best-selling Wisdom Books and 70 Teaching Tape Series.

2 **Church Crusades** - Multitudes are ministered to in crusades and seminars throughout America in "The Uncommon Wisdom Conference." Known as a man who loves pastors has focused on church crusades for 36 years.

3 **Music Ministry** - Millions have been blessed by the anointed songwriting and singing of Mike Murdock, who has made over 15 music albums and CDs available.

4 **Television** - *"Wisdom Keys With Mike Murdock,"* a nationally-syndicated weekly television program features Mike Murdock's teaching and music.

5 **The Wisdom Center** - The Ministry Offices where Dr. Murdock holds an annual School of Wisdom for those desiring "The Uncommon Life."

6 **Schools of the Holy Spirit** - Mike Murdock hosts Schools of the Holy Spirit in many churches to mentor believers on the Person and Companionship of the Holy Spirit.

7 **Schools of Wisdom** - In 24 major cities Mike Murdock hosts Saturday Schools of Wisdom for those who want personalized and advanced training for achieving "The Uncommon Life."

8 **Missionary Ministry** - Dr Mike. Murdock's overseas outreaches to 38 countries have included crusades in East and West Africa, South America and Europe.

My Gift Of Appreciation...
The Wisdom Commentary

The Wisdom Commentary includes 52 topics...for mentoring your family every week of the year.

These topics include:

- Abilities
- Achievement
- Anointing
- Assignment
- Bitterness
- Blessing
- Career
- Change
- Children
- Dating
- Depression
- Discipline
- Divorce
- Dreams And Goals
- Enemy
- Enthusiasm
- Favor
- Finances
- Fools

- Giving
- Goal-Setting
- God
- Happiness
- Holy Spirit
- Ideas
- Intercession
- Jobs
- Loneliness
- Love
- Mentorship
- Ministers
- Miracles
- Mistakes
- Money
- Negotiation
- Prayer
- Problem-Solving
- Protégés

- Satan
- Secret Place
- Seed-Faith
- Self-Confidence
- Struggle
- Success
- Time-Management
- Understanding
- Victory
- Weaknesses
- Wisdom
- Word Of God
- Words
- Work

THE *Mike Murdock* COLLECTOR'S EDITION

The Wisdom Commentary of MIKE MURDOCK

THE WISDOM COMMENTARY 1

VOLUME 1

My Gift Of Appreciation To My Sponsors!
..Those Who Sponsor One Square Foot In
The Completion Of The Wisdom Center!

Thank you so much for becoming a part of this wonderful project...The completion of The Wisdom Center! The total purchase and renovation cost of this facility (10,000 square feet) is just over $1,000,000. This is approximately $100 per square foot. **The Wisdom Commentary is my Gift of Appreciation for your Sponsorship Seed of $100...that sponsors one square foot of The Wisdom Center. Become a Sponsor!** You will love this Volume 1, of The Wisdom Commentary. It is my exclusive Gift of Appreciation for The Wisdom Key Family who partners with me in the Work of God as a Sponsor.

THE WISDOM CENTER
P.O. Box 99, Denton, Texas 76202

Website:
WWW.THEWISDOMCENTER.CC

**1-888-WISDOM1
(1-888-947-3661)**

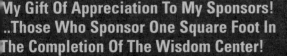

What Matters Most.

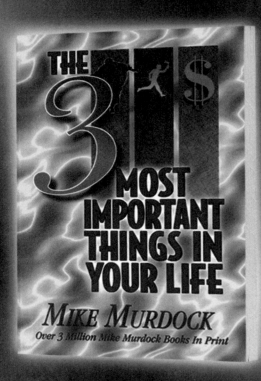

▶ 17 Facts You Should Know About The Holy Spirit

▶ The Greatest Weapon The Holy Spirit Has Given You

▶ 15 Facts About The Love Of The Holy Spirit

▶ 17 Facts Every Christian Should Know About Grieving The Holy Spirit

▶ 17 Facts You Should Know About The Anointing

▶ 3 Ways The Holy Spirit Will Talk To You

▶ 8 Important Facts About Your Assignment

The Holy Spirit, The Assignment, and The Seed. These three vital areas are the most important things in your life. Mike Murdock addresses each topic in a profound and dynamic way. In this volume he carefully lays out the Wisdom Secrets to Successful Living. Your understanding will be energized as knowledge enters your heart and you begin to find your Assignment in the purpose of God.

Wisdom Is The Principal Thing

Book B-101 / $10

The Wisdom Center

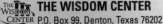

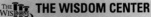

My Gift Of Appreciation...
The Wisdom Commentary

The Wisdom Commentary includes 52 topics...for mentoring your family every week of the year.

These topics include:

- Abilities
- Achievement
- Anointing
- Assignment
- Bitterness
- Blessing
- Career
- Change
- Children
- Dating
- Depression
- Discipline
- Divorce
- Dreams And Goals
- Enemy
- Enthusiasm
- Favor
- Finances
- Fools

- Giving
- Goal-Setting
- God
- Happiness
- Holy Spirit
- Ideas
- Intercession
- Jobs
- Loneliness
- Love
- Mentorship
- Ministers
- Miracles
- Mistakes
- Money
- Negotiation
- Prayer
- Problem-Solving
- Protégés

- Satan
- Secret Place
- Seed-Faith
- Self-Confidence
- Struggle
- Success
- Time-Management
- Understanding
- Victory
- Weaknesses
- Wisdom
- Word Of God
- Words
- Work

THE *Mike Murdock* COLLECTOR'S EDITION

THE WISDOM COMMENTARY 1

Gift Of Appreciation
For Your Sponsorship Seed of $100 or More
Gift Of Appreciation

My Gift Of Appreciation To My Sponsors!
...Those Who Sponsor One Square Foot In The Completion Of The Wisdom Center!

Thank you so much for becoming a part of this wonderful project...The completion of The Wisdom Center! The total purchase and renovation cost of this facility (10,000 square feet) is just over $1,000,000. This is approximately $100 per square foot. **The Wisdom Commentary is my Gift of Appreciation for your Sponsorship Seed of $100...that sponsors one square foot of The Wisdom Center. Become a Sponsor!** You will love this Volume 1, of The Wisdom Commentary. It is my exclusive Gift of Appreciation for The Wisdom Key Family who partners with me in the Work of God as a Sponsor.

Add 10% For S/H

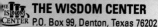
THE WISDOM CENTER
P.O. Box 99, Denton, Texas 76202

1-888-WISDOM1
(1-888-947-3661)

Website:
WWW.THEWISDOMCENTER.TV

c

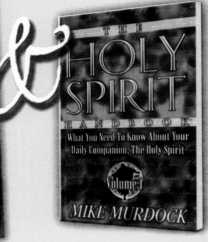

Master Secrets To Uncommon Increase.

The Lord God Of Your Fathers Make You A Thousand Times So Many More As You Are, And Bless You, As He Hath Promised You! Deuteronomy 1:11

MURDOCK

31 REASONS PEOPLE DO NOT RECEIVE THEIR FINANCIAL HARVEST

MIKE MURDOCK

THE WISDOM CENTER
MIKE MURDOCK • P.O. Box 99 • Denton, Texas

7 KEYS to 1000 TIMES MORE

The Wisdom Center

6 Tapes | $30
TS-104
PAK-008
Wisdom Is The Principal Thing

The Wisdom Center

Free Book
B-82 ($12 Value)
Enclosed!
Wisdom Is The Principal Thing

The Greatest Success Law I Ever Discovered
7 Reasons God Wants To Increase Your Finances
58 Important Facts About Obedience

Add 10% For S/H

 **THE WISDOM CENTER**
P.O. Box 99, Denton, Texas 76202

1-888-WISDOM1
(1-888-947-3661)

Website:
WWW.THEWISDOMCENTER.TV

E

SCHOOL of WISDOM #2

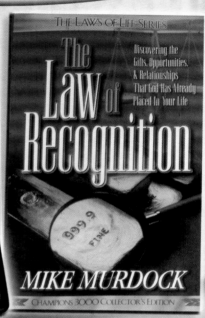

The Law of Recognition — Discovering the Gifts, Opportunities, & Relationships That God Has Already Placed In Your Life

MIKE MURDOCK — Champions 3000 Collector's Edition

DR. MIKE MURDOCK
The School of Wisdom

▶ 47 Keys In Recognizing The Mate God Has Approved For You

▶ 14 Facts You Should Know About Your Gifts and Talents

▶ 17 Important Facts You Should Remember About Your Weakness

▶ And Much, Much More...

▶ What Attracts Others Toward You

▶ The Secret Of Multiplying Your Financial Blessings

▶ What Stops The Flow Of Your Faith

▶ Why Some Fail And Others Succeed

▶ How To Discern Your Life Assignment

▶ How To Create Currents Of Favor With Others

▶ How To Defeat Loneliness

The Wisdom Center
6 Tapes | $30
TS-90
PAK-002
Wisdom Is The Principal Thing

The Wisdom Center
Free Book
B-114 ($10 Value)
ENCLOSED!
Wisdom Is The Principal Thing

Add 10% For S/H

THE WISDOM CENTER
P.O. Box 99, Denton, Texas 76202

1-888-WISDOM1
(1-888-947-3661)

Website:
WWW.THEWISDOMCENTER.TV